THE
GREAT RESCVE

Books by Edward William Fudge

The Sound of His Voice

The Great Rescue

Two Views of Hell (co-author)

The Fire That Consumes

THE
GREAT RESCUE

the story of
God's amazing grace

EDWARD WILLIAM FUDGE

New
Leaf
Books

ORANGE, CAIFORNIA

THE GREAT RESCUE: The Story of God's Amazing Grace
published by New Leaf Books

Copyright © 2002 by Edward William Fudge

ISBN 0-9714289-3-X
Printed in the United States of America

Cover design by Mark Cole, ColeGrafix

For information:
New Leaf Books, 12542 S. Fairmont, Orange, CA 92869
1-877-634-6004 (toll free)

Visit our website: www.newleafbooks.org

10 9 8 7 6 5 4 3 2 1   08 07 06 05 04 03 02

DEDICATED TO

Julia Taylor Simpson,
beloved grandchild.

CONTENTS

THE REALIZATION

THE RESULTS

ACKNOWLEDGEMENTS

To my friend and publisher, Leonard Allen,
for suggesting this book, for prayer support during its writing,
and for skillful labor in its production and presentation;

To Al Haley and Sara Fudge,
who read the manuscript and made helpful suggestions
for its improvement;

To Jeremy Fudge,
who spent many hours discussing content as well as style,
and whose detailed editing is as invisible as it is valuable;

To my Sunday night group, for their encouragement; and

To all from throughout the Church universal
who have taught me the Bible and its Story,
in person, through their own writings,
and by their lived examples —

I thank you and thank God for your gifts.

The Author

Foreword

Edward Fudge proves himself to be an enormously gifted storyteller in this fresh and robust account of *The Great Rescue*. The rescue around which the story turns is nothing less than the redemptive activity of the God of the Universe who "seeks out his errant human creatures and brings them back to himself." It is a story as ancient as the opening pages of the Bible, yet it will touch every reader with fresh relevance and power.

It would be hard to imagine a more compelling story. *The Great Rescue* breathes excitement, pathos, mystery—all of the qualities of great drama. And yet at the same time it unfolds for the reader, whether biblical sophisticate or novice, the basic truths about God's grand purpose for the people he created for His own joy.

The book is at once a gripping story (it will be hard to put down once it's opened) and a compelling theology text. Here unfolds the sweeping panorama of God's redemptive work, taking the reader literally from Genesis to Revelation. The resulting picture is truly a masterpiece of grace, in which the author as artist paints with strokes sometimes bold and sometimes finely detailed. Biblical truths on which our very lives hang are made accessible to readers of every level. And, certainly, the reader will surely be lead back to the Bible itself with fresh insight and expectancy.

From the riveting profile of an utterly broken and lost world that fills the first page, to the crescendo of salvation that rings throughout, *The Great Rescue* reaches its climax in a stunning final chapter that is itself worth the price of the book.

Fudge has the capacity to crystallize biblical concepts, large and small, into a gripping story line that both captures the imagination and teaches profound truth. Without getting bogged down in theological distinctions that would only distract, he nevertheless unfolds the central doctrines of the Bible with precision and accuracy that will leave the reader enthralled with the God who is behind it all. In truth, the only possible response at the final word will be a response of worship.

> *James E. Sweeney*
> *Provost & Professor of Pastoral Theology*
> *Western Seminary*
> *Portland, Oregon*

One

OUR PROBLEM

Our Broken World

Human beings everywhere sense that things are not as they ought to be. Every place we look, we see signs of a broken world. Babies die and children starve. Adults fight, torture and enslave each other. Ethnic neighbors who co-existed peacefully for generations suddenly massacre one other instead. Totalitarian rulers attack believers, persecute dissidents, and forbid independent thought.

AIDS—the modern Black Plague—ravages less-developed countries and woefully affects the world. Advanced nations watch helplessly as heart attacks topple, accidents cripple and catastrophic diseases strike down. Children and adults go on killing sprees. Terrorists maim and mangle. Murders, rapes and missing children fill the evening news.

In pursuit of progress, we foul the water, destroy the forests and pollute the air. We work harder and longer in our quest for a better life, only to discover that we have grown a monster we cannot afford to feed. We desire rest but generate stress. We sacrifice our lives to obtain a living. In the process, we lose our families and forget who we really are.

So we build hospitals and hospices. We construct prisons and jails. We read the experts, retain lawyers, consult psychologists and counselors—but it is all too little and too late. We can punish but we cannot prevent. At best, we can only hope to minimize the damage, contain the violence, limit the destruction of our bodies, minds, homes, societies and earth. No, things are not as they ought to be.

The Darkest Day

But none of these calamities, as horrible as they surely are, fully portrays the true brokenness of our world. To see that picture, we must travel nearly two centuries back in time, to a place still marked by conflict, hate and revenge. We must go to Jerusalem—outside the city limits—to a place called Golgotha and Calvary. There we encounter a public execution in progress.

Brutal business. It is a busy scene, and a noisy one besides. We hear the ring of a heavy wooden mallet as it strikes a hard metal spike. Screams and cursing fill the air. More hammering. There are cries of sadness ... and of pain. The small crowd is mixed—Roman soldiers, a few Pharisees, a host of commoners. Women wail and soldiers jeer. A few minutes pass. It is a bit quieter now. We look up. There, beside this public roadway, stand three crosses. On them are nailed the tortured bodies of three, still-living men. Pilate, the Roman occupation official, has sentenced them to this slow and torturous death.

Two of the men, whose names we do not know, are notable criminals—convicted highwaymen, armed robbers (Matt. 27:38). One of them says it aloud: they deserve the punishment they now endure (Luke 23:39-41). But between these outlaws hangs Jesus of Nazareth. "What is he doing here?" you ask. To the Jewish onlooker that day, the question pressed with even greater weight. This sight is not only tragic, it is absolutely immoral. For Jesus is no unknown figure, and everything we know about him is good.

Innocence executed. The Nazarene is a teacher of the Torah, although he never attended the rabbinical schools. For three years now, his reputation has spread throughout the land of Israel. Citizens from the seaport villages of Galilee in the north to this capital city of Jerusalem have watched him closely and have discussed him among themselves. The common people admire his wise words. They respect him for his courage in standing up to the Pharisees. They love him for his compassionate deeds.

Eyewitnesses excitedly reported how he brought back to life dead Lazarus of Bethany, the daughter of the Jewish official Jairus, and that poor widow's son during the funeral procession in the little village of Nain (John 11:38-44; Mark 5:22-42; Luke 7:11-17). Whole towns in Galilee and in Judea saw him heal their sick, expel demons and make lepers suddenly whole.

At Jesus' word, say those who saw it, paralyzed people stood up and walked—some even danced in the street for joy. Others, long known to be blind, suddenly regained their sight (Mark 1:32-2:12; 8:22-26). One day as Jesus was teaching in the countryside, with thousands of villagers eagerly pressing round him to hear, he broke five barley-loaves and two small fishes and fed them all (John 6:5-14).

Even his enemies admit that Jesus has never hurt anyone. His Jewish adversaries accuse him of blasphemy, for he has claimed to be God's promised Messiah. When challenged point-blank, however, none of them can convict him of any wrong (John 8:46). Pilate, the Roman procurator, three times declared Jesus to be innocent of all charges, and publicly washed his hands as he turned Jesus over to the executioners (Luke 23:20-22).

How, we wonder, can these things be happening? Why is Jesus on that cross? Why is he not screaming back at those who taunt him and mock him? How can he possibly pray for their forgiveness—as someone standing near his cross says they overheard? What is wrong with this world? What is wrong with God? Does God even exist? If he does exist, where is he now?

The suffering and death of Jesus Christ show us, more than any other event or word throughout history, that something is dreadfully wrong with our world and with our human race. That "something," the Bible tells us, is sin.

The Bible reveals much more about our sinfulness and our sins, and we will examine some of that revelation in the following chapter. But nothing reveals more clearly the extent of our problem, the depth of our sinfulness, the breadth of our malaise, than the public exposure of sin's true character as revealed at Calvary. There we see the genuine reflection of our own sin. There we see its ultimate result. There—as strange as it may seem—we also see its only remedy, reversal and cure. This cure, we shall discover, involves families, society and the very heavens and earth.

Two

In the Beginning

We do not need the Bible to tell us that our world is broken through and through—from our innermost selves to our relationships with each other, even the physical planet itself. How this brokenness occurred, and why, we cannot determine—either by intuition or by observation. For that information we need the Bible, which practically starts at that point. "Practically starts," we say, because that is actually the second story in Genesis and not the first.

From Chaos to Cosmos

The Bible opens with God creating the universe—"the heavens and the earth," to use the ancient Hebrew phrase. The next sentence tells us that the earth is formless and empty. Darkness covers it all. However, this scene is soon to change, for the Spirit of God is hovering over the dark and watery waste. Chaos is about to encounter the Creator!

Throughout the rest of Genesis 1, God replaces primeval chaos with order and beauty. First, God forms what has been formless. He distinguishes the elements, arranging and adorning a whole world (cosmos) of day and night, of subterranean waters and airy skies, of dry land and seas. Next, God fills what has been empty. Plants and trees sprout across the dry land.

Sun, moon and stars begin to sparkle in the heavens. Fish and sea creatures play in the water. Birds chirp and flutter in the air. Beasts explore their new habitat. Crawling creatures scurry on the ground. Cattle contentedly stand and graze.

Finally, God crowns his creation with human beings—male and female, in extraordinary variety. He appoints them as stewards of the earth, which he has newly formed and filled. Then, with an infinite eye and divine wisdom, God reviews his creation and declares it "very good." That said, the Creator takes a day off to rest and to enjoy what he has made.

A World in Harmony

After telling the story of this week in the life of God, Genesis gives another summary of the creation, "in the day that the LORD God made earth and heaven" (Gen. 2:4-25). Whether this is a second biblical version of affairs or simply a close-up look at the details involving animals and humans is not important. What are important are the details this story provides. Males and females share a special unity, we learn here. God puts them together in marriage as husband and wife. And these first two start out in innocence, the man Adam ("Clay-man") and the woman Eve ("Living Mother").

This story also places Adam and Eve in a paradise called the Garden of Eden. Here, God gives Adam permission to eat from every fruit tree that grows—with one exception. The tree in the center of the Garden is off limits. God calls it "the tree of the knowledge of good and evil." This is a symbolic name, composed of Hebrew idioms. It roughly means "the tree of moral awareness learned by actual experience." Through this tree, God will see whether the human creatures will take his word regarding what is good and bad, or whether they will decide to find that out for themselves. They can obey God and continue to live in an innocent Paradise. Or they can disobey God, spoil it all and eventually die.

At this point, the scene is so wonderful we think we must be dreaming. None of us has ever seen such a place. Human beings frolic in an unspoiled world, walking and talking with the Creator himself. The animal kingdom is at peace, without bloodshed by man or beast. Adam and Eve live in harmony with nature, caring for creation and enjoying its beauty and fruitfulness. They nurture each other without competition, their individual gifts perfectly matched to the other's need. There is no sin in the world—no sickness or sorrow or human death.

No wonder God called it "very good." But God has given the human creatures the opportunity to choose. The future of the world, it appears, is now in their creaturely hands.

Humans Rebel Against the Creator

Here the story moves forward, in the original Hebrew, with a playful pun. Since they have no reason for shameful self-consciousness, Adam and Eve are naked—literally "slick" (Gen. 2:25). But there is another "slick" (translated "crafty") creature in the Garden. This one is a talking serpent, which begins to entice the woman with the pleasures awaiting her in the fruit from that tree in the center of the Garden. The New Testament identifies this serpent as the Devil, also called Satan—himself a fallen angel and the instigator of evil on this earth (Rev. 12:9; 20:2). In the end, Eve eats the forbidden fruit, as does Adam, and all that was good begins to unravel before their eyes (Gen. 3:6-24).

Suddenly the first humans experience a sensation that they have never felt before. It is guilt. For the first time in their lives, they sense a separation from their Creator. They also realize that their relationship with each other is now fractured. Instead of protecting Eve and defending her, Adam blames Eve for his own wrong decision. Productivity takes on the new dimension of pain—in Adam's gardening and in Eve's childbearing.

A curse has fallen on creation. Earth itself is now out of kilter with the Creator as the result of human rebellion. In the following chapters of Genesis, Adam's son, Cain, kills his brother Abel. Civilization develops while morality declines, and God finally judges the world with a great Flood but graciously delivers one faithful man, Noah, and his immediate family (Gen. 4-9).

Ironically, Adam and Eve found what they looked for—"knowing good and evil" (Gen. 3:22). But it was not what they expected. So long as their knowledge came from trusting and obeying God's word, they had enjoyed a glorious Paradise. The Creator had been their friend and they had welcomed his companionship.

When Adam and Eve decided to determine "good and evil" for themselves, without regard to God's word, they disrupted the moral harmony of the universe and triggered a cosmic ruin. Because they had become unfit to live forever in their broken condition, God banished Adam and Eve from the Garden, and from access to another tree with a name signifying fellowship with God. That symbolic name is the Tree of Life (Gen. 3:22-24). We will encounter it again at the end of the larger Story.

Although Adam and Eve both sinned by eating the forbidden fruit, the Bible writers generally blame Adam, whom they view as rebellious, more than they do Eve, whom they view as naïve (2 Cor. 11:3; 1 Tim. 2:14). "So Adam sinned in the Garden," you might say. "What does that have to do with me?" Very much indeed, the Bible tells us—and we confirm what it says by our own experience and observation every day.

Three

ALL IN THE FAMILY

Two Images

When God first made Adam and Eve, he made them "in the image of God" (Gen. 1:26-27). Theologians have written whole books on the meaning of that phrase, and we certainly cannot explain here all that it might involve. This much, however, seems certain: God planned humans for fellowship with himself, and he created Adam and Eve with that potential and for that purpose.

Morally, Adam was totally free. He could choose to sin—and follow through with it. Or he could choose not to sin—and carry out that good decision. The first human couple was not predisposed to do what was wrong. Had they wished to do so, Adam and Eve could have lived forever in obedience to God, trusting the Creator as dependent creatures should. They could have eaten regularly from the fruit of the Tree of Life and enjoyed ongoing intimacy with God in an untarnished world.

Sadly, that state of innocence, of unhindered moral ability, died with our first parents. Genesis signifies this fact almost in passing. Adam and Eve are made in the likeness of God, but the next human generation, represented by their third son Seth, is made in Adam's own likeness and according to his image

(Gen. 5:1-3). Like Seth, every other human has also carried the fallen likeness of our original ancestor. Jesus Christ, the Son of God and the Last Adam, is the only exception. Adam's sin forfeited Paradise, marred the image of God, and plunged the human race into sin.

There is more to the matter than this, but Adam's sin set a bad example that every person capable of choice has followed, except Jesus Christ. Hosea might have spoken of humankind in general when he said of his countrymen that "like Adam they have transgressed" (Hos. 6:7). Long before Hosea, the Psalmist had observed: "There is not one who does good, not even one" (Ps. 14:3). Centuries later, the Apostle Paul similarly concluded that "all have sinned, and fall short of the glory of God" (Rom. 3:23). That indictment is true regardless of national origin or racial heritage. It is true regardless of the nature, content or degree of spiritual revelation that anyone has from God (Rom. 1:18-3:23).

Why, you might ask, does everyone who is capable of making moral decisions end up choosing to do what is wrong? Why is sin so universal? What has happened to the human race? The Old Testament identifies the problem in the fallen human heart—a biblical figure of speech for the combined intellect, emotions and will of a woman or a man. "The heart is more deceitful than all else and is desperately sick," writes Jeremiah. "Who can understand it?" (Jer. 17:9.) Since Adam, sin is inherent in our human race. It is as native to our natural self as spots are native to a leopard (Jer. 13:23). That is the way we are born (Ps. 51:5; 58:3).

Adam Our Representative

What the Old Testament only hints in this regard, the New Testament reveals and explains. The Apostle Paul discusses Adam's relationship to the human race in detail, in Romans 5. Paul's comments sound strange to our Western democratic minds, used to thinking in individualistic terms. However, his concepts were far more familiar to those who first read his letter. In ancient times and even today, Middle Eastern people thought in terms of the group, the tribe, the People. One individual often represents an entire clan, especially if that individual is a founding father of the group. This is the way Paul views Adam's sin and its consequences on the human race.

The stark reality. Paul begins his discussion with a startling affirmation. "Through one man sin entered into the world, and death through sin, and so death spread to all men, because all sinned" (Rom. 5:12). Before Adam sinned, there was no human sin in the world. Because Adam sinned, sin came into the world with death at its heels. In this way, death became the destiny of all Adam's descendants, because they all sinned in Adam. This is Paul's strong announcement, as difficult as it might be for us to hear.

But wait, you say—death came to all people because each of them personally sinned, not because Adam sinned as their representative. Paul seems to have anticipated this very comment, so he explains his bold statement in the verses immediately following.

"For," he begins in verse 13. ("For" means "because," and it tells us that an explanation is on the way.) "For until the Law [of Moses] sin was in the world; but sin is not imputed when there is no law. Nevertheless death reigned from Adam until Moses, even over those who had not sinned in the likeness of Adam's offense" (verses 12-14).

It is clear that everyone sinned in Adam, Paul is saying, because God does not count sin against someone who had no specific command to violate. After Adam, God did not give a specific law until he gave the Law through Moses. Yet every generation between Adam and Moses also died. This means that they violated God's specific command—and they did so in Adam their representative when he ate the forbidden fruit.

The sad results. Notice Paul's sobering description in Romans 5 of the results of Adam's sin:

- "by the transgression of the one, the many died" (v. 15)
- "the judgment arose from one transgression, resulting in condemnation" (v. 16)
- "by the transgression of the one, death reigned through the one" (v. 17)
- "through one transgression there resulted condemnation to all men" (v. 18)
- "through the one man's disobedience the many were made sinners" (v. 19).

Because Adam was our representative, the head of our human clan, what he did counted for us. Because we were "in Adam," what he did, we also did. Because of Adam's original rebellion against God, manifested in his decision to eat the forbidden fruit, the whole human race (except Jesus) became sinners—sinners who sin, who eventually die and who stand condemned before God.

If the Great Rescuer had not come, every descendant of Adam would have remained in that exact condition, totally without hope. And, as dark as that scene may be, the full reality is even more gloomy that that.

Four

REALITY SHOCKS

A Fallen Nature

This, then, is why we all make bad choices. We have a fallen nature, which the Apostle Paul frequently calls "the flesh," and it is prone to sin. We are naturally inclined to violate God's commands, to choose our own will instead of his will. It is not the way God created the human race, but it is the way the human race became after that original sin. We know by experience that this is true of ourselves, and we know by observation that it is true of others.

No matter how sweet we look as babies, there is a nature inside us that is fallen and bent toward doing wrong. We prove this as soon as we learn how. Even as children, our instinctive response to a command is to violate it. One of our earliest words is a defiant "no." Like Adam, we break the rules. As we grow older, this reality only becomes clearer. Sin has power over us, in every aspect of our being. Our intellect is fallen, for we imagine evil thoughts. Our emotions are fallen, for we love what is evil and hate what is good. Our will is fallen, for we choose to do what is wrong.

Spiritually sick. We are spiritually diseased through and through. The words of the ancient Hebrew prophet Isaiah tell the truth about us all:

The whole head is sick,
  And the whole heart is faint.
From the sole of the foot even to the head
  There is nothing sound in it.
Only bruises, welts, and raw wounds,
  Not pressed out or bandaged,
  Nor softened with oil (Isa. 1:5-6).

We try to forget our evil thoughts, words and deeds, and to pretend that we are pure. But God—who knows every thought we think, hears every word we say, and sees every hidden or open deed—has a different opinion. In his sight, we are not clean and pure at all. We are more like an unwashed and abandoned baby, discovered in a ditch, filthy and squirming in its blood (Ezek. 16:1-5). It is a shocking and graphic comparison, but we sometimes need to be shocked into reality.

God looks down from heaven and sees a human race that is "foolish, disobedient, deceived, enslaved to various lusts and pleasures, spending life in malice and envy, hateful, hating one another" (Titus 3:3). Because of our sin—both in Adam and in our own wrong choices—we are cut off from God, without hope in the world (Eph. 2:12). Even those of us born into Christian homes, who grew up "in the church," are part of this motley lot. Together, we all have been "bound up" in disobedience (Rom. 11:32, *NIV*)—a verb used elsewhere of fish helplessly caught in a net (Luke 5:6). No fallen human being dares to stand before God and ask for what he or she deserves (Luke 18:9-14).

No help within ourselves. Because we are fallen through and through, we possess no faculty or power that can lift us back to the Creator. We cannot reason or think ourselves into God's fellowship, for our intellect is fallen. We cannot reach God through self-confidence, self-anger or self-pity, for our emotions are fallen, too. We cannot eliminate our sin-prone nature and our own record of wrongs by making correct decisions, for our will is fallen as well.

If moral muscle could fix our sin, we would still be broken, for we are morally "helpless" (Rom. 5:6). If goodness could solve our problem, it would not help, for we are really "sinners" (Rom. 5:8). If cooperation with God were the solution, it would do us no good, for we are actually at odds with him instead (Rom. 5:10).

We are like a paralyzed man in a wheelchair trapped on the fifth floor of a burning building. The stairs are blazing, the elevators disabled and the halls are filled with suffocating smoke. The man has no mask to put on, no protective gear to wear, and no fire escape to descend. The man is utterly helpless to help himself.

Spiritually dead. The Bible sees our condition as worse than paralyzed. We are "dead" in our sinful state (Eph. 2:1-2). We do not need spiritual formulas, religious conditions or moral rules. Even if we had them, they would do us no good. A dead person cannot obey rules, meet conditions or follow formulas. In our natural, fallen condition, we are already under God's wrath (Eph. 2:3). We fancy that we can see the path to life, but in reality we are spiritually blind (John 9:41). We imagine that we can freely choose to do what is right, but the truth is that we are helplessly enslaved by sin (John 8:34).

We cannot remedy our helpless situation. We cannot offer any relief and we cannot provide a cure. If we are ever to be rescued from sin—from its penalty, its power or its presence—something or someone outside ourselves must provide that deliverance. "What are we to do with this news?" you ask. "Why discuss a situation over which I have no control?"

The answer is that we must face the truth about our situation. For until we know our spiritual helplessness, we will imagine that we can save ourselves. Until we acknowledge that we are spiritually dead, we will tell ourselves that we can climb back up to God. We will pretend that we can please God by doing good, or by doing our part. We will imagine that we can contribute something toward our own salvation.

Impossible and possible. Jesus' followers once asked him a very important question: "Who can be saved?" Jesus made two short statements in response. His first comment surely chills us to the bone. "With men," said Jesus, "this is impossible." Impossible! Let it sink in.

Our age goes to great lengths to avoid facing this truth. Not only do irreligious and unchurched people avoid this truth. So, very often, church members and leaders, Bible teachers and preachers, do as well. But we must hear and acknowledge this "impossible." Only when we accept it are we ready to hear Jesus' second comment—a word of hope for helpless people. "But with God," Jesus continued, "all things are possible" (Matt. 19:25-26).

The God who created the universe from nothing can also rescue his fallen creation. But a rescue operation this large and complex calls for careful planning and preparation— even for the God who does the impossible. The Jewish Scriptures, which Christians include as the first three-fourths of their own Bible and call the "Old Testament," tell the story of that preparation.

If you already know the Old Testament story, think of these next three chapters as a memory freshener. If that part of the Bible is new to you, or if your acquaintance with it occurred long ago, this short summary will give you the big picture. The Old Testament story is simple, but it is very important. In fact, trying to understand the New Testament without any knowledge of the Old is like walking into a two-hour movie with only thirty minutes left to run.

On the surface, this is the story of Israel as God's chosen people. Because the Israelites are God's *people,* their story includes all the problems, temptations, struggles and failures common to humankind. These are very ordinary people, sinners like all of us. But Israel is *God's* people—and that makes all the difference. Although this is Israel's story, it is crisscrossed with divine footprints—footprints that lead us through the centuries, straight to the Great Rescue. Of course, there were no road signs that explained these footprints at the time. Their destination and deeper meaning would become clear only in retrospect, in the light of later events.

Five

GOD CREATES A PEOPLE

Abraham's 'Impossible' Son

Abram. The story of Israel begins in ancient Mesopotamia—located in Iraq on today's world globe—about 2,000 years before the birth of Jesus Christ. One day, quite out of the blue, God speaks to a man named Abram, who lives in a city called Ur of the Chaldees. God tells Abram to pack his bags, tell his relatives goodbye and leave Ur for a land that God will show him. He also promises to make Abram famous, to make his descendants into a great nation and to bless "all the families of the earth" through him.

In Abram's day, archaeology tells us, Ur is a developed city, having the ancient equivalent of tract homes and courtyards. Its residents use razors and mirrors, and even enjoy running water. Despite these conveniences, Abram assembles his caravan as God commanded and begins a journey without a map, eventually arriving in the Land of Canaan. God appears to Abram again and promises to give his descendants this land—later known as Palestine and as Israel.

Isaac. God also promises Abram, who has no children, that he will have descendants too numerous to count. This promise is humanly impossible because of Abram's advanced age and that of his wife, Sarai. Nevertheless, Abram believes God (literally, he says "Amen"), and God declares Abram to be in good standing with the Creator. Years pass, until Abram (now "Abraham") is 100 years old and his wife (now "Sarah") is 90. Then, just as God promised, Abraham and Sarah have a son. They name him Isaac.

Isaac grows into a young man and Abraham happily considers God's promises concerning Isaac's future. Then one day God tells Abraham to take his son to a particular mountain and offer him as a burnt sacrifice to God. The command seems to contradict God's earlier promises, and it certainly goes against Abraham's fatherly love for his son, but the old patriarch sets out to obey this harsh command. Isaac carries the wood for the fire. Just as Abraham is about to plunge a knife into his son, however, God stops the action and shows Abraham a ram to sacrifice instead. Abraham names the place Yahweh-Jireh, which means "The LORD Will Provide."

A Son Becomes a Clan

Jacob. Isaac grows up, marries his cousin Rebekah, and they have twin sons, Jacob and Esau. Esau is born first, with Jacob clutching his heel. As the two grow to manhood, Jacob continues to grab what belongs to Esau. Jacob first deceives their blind father into giving him Isaac's gift of the ancestral blessing. Later, he coerces Esau out of his birthright—the older son's customary entitlement to a prize portion of the family inheritance. When Esau threatens to kill Jacob, Jacob flees to his mother's original homeland of Haran.

In Haran, Jacob marries his two cousins, Rachel and Leah, and takes their two female servants as concubines. He works for his father-in-law Laban for a period of twenty years, each man constantly trying to take advantage of the other. Jacob accumulates massive flocks and herds, then abruptly leaves Haran and returns to Canaan. Along the way, Jacob confronts God, who changes his name from Jacob to Israel. He also encounters his brother Esau, with whom he makes peace. With his four wives and concubines, Jacob has twelve sons and one daughter.

Joseph. Jacob's favorite child is Joseph, the son of his favorite wife, Rachel. Joseph's brothers grow to hate him, however, as they observe Jacob's obvious favoritism, and as Joseph tells them his own dreams in which the brothers always show Joseph special respect and honor. One day when their shepherding has them all far from home, the jealous brothers abandon Joseph in a dry well, then sell him to a caravan of traders on their way to Egypt.

In Egypt, the traders sell Joseph to Pharoah's security chief, a man named Potiphar. When Joseph repels the repeated sexual advances of Potiphar's wife, she falsely accuses Joseph of attempted rape, and Potiphar has Joseph imprisoned. After several years, God enables Joseph to translate Pharoah's prophetic dreams, and Joseph becomes second-in-command over all of Egypt. A famine falls on the Land of Canaan and Jacob sends Joseph's brothers to Egypt to buy grain.

Joseph, whom his brothers do not recognize, accuses them of espionage and holds one brother hostage while the others return to their father Jacob. The dramatic story concludes with Joseph rescuing his father's family—seventy adults plus children—from famine and relocating them in Egypt. Generations pass and Jacob's descendants become the Egyptians' slaves—setting the stage for the greatest rescue, or salvation story, of the Old Testament.

Moses, the Would-Be Rescuer

The world has seen many instances of slavery, and of liberation from bondage. But only the Children of Israel—also known as the Hebrews, after the name of Eber, an ancient ancestor—have stood helplessly by and watched while their God single-handedly overthrew the oppressor and set his people free.

This mighty deliverance is the defining story of the Old Testament Scriptures. Not until the Great Rescue itself will God perform a greater saving deed.

With the passing of generations, the Hebrews multiply into more than a million population. The Egyptian Pharoah, or king, senses in Israel a potential ally for Egypt's enemies. In desperation, Pharoah orders the Egyptian midwives to kill every newborn Hebrew boy. But the midwives fear God and disobey the king. Finally, Pharoah orders the Hebrews to throw every newborn son into the Nile River, but to keep the daughters alive.

A defiant mother. A year or more goes by and one Hebrew mother decides to defy the king's order. For three months, she hides her baby at home. Then, perhaps because he becomes too noisy to hide safely, she makes a wicker basket, lays her baby in the floating crib and places it among the reeds by the bank of the Nile. The mother returns home, but the baby's older sister waits nearby to see what will occur. This is the place where the Egyptian princess regularly comes to bathe.

As expected, the king's daughter discovers the baby and decides to adopt him as her own son. Unaware of their identities and at the suggestion of the baby's sister, the princess hires the baby's own mother to care for the child. The princess names her adopted son Moses. Moses grows up, enjoying all the privileges that belong to the son of Pharoah's daughter.

Moses frees and flees. One day, after Moses is grown, he sees an Egyptian beating a slave. Moses kills the Egyptian and buries him in the sand. Pharoah learns what Moses has done and tries to kill him in return, but Moses escapes from Egypt and hides in the country of Midian. In Midian, Moses rescues seven sisters from harassment at a community well. The sisters are daughters of Jethro, a Midianite priest, who becomes Moses' father-in-law.

Moses, who once envisioned himself as a deliverer, becomes a shepherd instead, tending Jethro's sheep. Moses pursues this

lonely wilderness occupation for 40 years, as his natural ambition and self-reliance slowly drain away. Meanwhile, back in
Egypt, the Pharoah dies. The oppressed Children of Israel sigh
under their hardships and cry out in despair.

A divine encounter. One day, as Moses pastures his flock
near Mount Horeb, also called Mount Sinai, an angel of God
appears to him in a blazing fire from the middle of a desert bush.
Moses watches the bush, which does not burn up. God speaks
to Moses from the bush, identifying himself as the God of
Abraham, Isaac and Jacob. He has heard the Hebrews' cries for
help in Egypt, God says, and he is ready to deliver them from
slavery. Then comes the startling announcement—God intends
to use Moses to accomplish this task.

The now-humbled Moses protests that he is unable to do
anything, and God assures Moses that he will go with him. At
this, Moses asks God's name. "I AM THAT I AM," God replies.
This mysterious phrase affirms that God is unlimited by time
and ability, and it signifies his ever-present power to save. God
also tells Moses his "memorial-name," the name which forever
reminds God's people of his covenant. It is a name without
vowels in Hebrew, a name so holy that the Jews do not pronounce it. In English letters, it is YHWH or JHVH—translated
sometimes as "Yahweh," "Jehovah" or "the LORD."

On his way to Egypt, Moses meets his brother Aaron, whom
God has sent to be his spokesman. When they arrive in Egypt,
Moses and Aaron call together the tribal elders of the Hebrews
and report all that God has said. The elders believe Moses and
worship God who has heard their cry for help. Moses and Aaron
tell Pharoah that Yahweh, the God of Israel commands: "Let my
people go." Pharoah, who is furious, refuses.

A power play of plagues. Moses and Aaron offer Pharoah a
second chance to obey God, but the king will hear nothing of
it. God then unleashes a series of ten plagues on the
Egyptians—a horrendous sequence of every natural catastrophe

that occasionally upset Egyptian life, plus other disasters the Egyptians would never imagine. The plagues demonstrate a supernatural source, supernatural timing, supernatural intensity and supernatural selectivity in target.

More than all that, however, the plagues represent warfare between Israel's God and all the gods of Egypt. For these plagues attack and disturb and destroy everything that the Egyptians worship and consider holy. They arrive to demonstrate that there is but one true God. He is Yahweh, the LORD, God of the Hebrews. Because of these plagues, his name will become known throughout the earth.

To begin with, the Nile River—the life-giving irrigation source for all of Egypt's crops—turns to blood, the universal symbol of death. The frogs leave their normal watery habitats and hop into houses, invading bedrooms and kitchens. Pesky insects—first as crawling larvae, then as buzzing flies—swarm everywhere throughout Egypt. Soon no location, indoor or out, is safe. Nowhere, that is, except the area of Goshen, where the Hebrew people live. From this plague forward, God distinguishes between the Egyptians, whom he afflicts in each case, and his own people, who remain unaffected.

Pharoah briefly relents in word, then changes his mind. Deadly disease kills Egypt's grazing livestock. Moses throws handfuls of soot into the air. As the wind carries the soot over Egypt, boils erupt on the bodies of the Egyptian people and their domestic animals. Moses repeats God's demand to Pharoah, whose heart God hardens, and Pharoah again refuses to obey.

The next day, a hailstorm strikes Egypt with a severity never before recorded. Pounding rain pummels the land. Lightning repeatedly strikes the earth. The storm kills even more of Egypt's remaining livestock and demolishes its agricultural harvest for that season. God tells Moses that there is more to come.

Moses again warns Pharoah, who again hardens his heart. For a night and a day, God sends an east wind over Egypt, bringing an invasion of locusts that cover the light of the sun. The locusts eat the few remaining crops, but they do not stop with that. They then fill the Egyptians' houses. Pharoah summons Moses and asks him to pray for God to halt the plague. Moses intercedes for Pharoah and God shifts the wind to blow the locusts out of Egypt. God again hardens stubborn Pharoah's heart, and the king does not let God's people go.

Moses next stretches out his hand and God sends a thick darkness over the land of Egypt—a darkness so dense that it can be felt. The Egyptians cannot leave their homes for the darkness, but the Children of Israel enjoy normal light. To the Egyptians, it appears that Ra, the sun-god, must have died. Not for one day only does Ra disappear, but for two days, and then for three. (When God brings about the Great Rescue centuries later, Satan seems to have remembered this humiliation, and tries to turn it back on God. The Great Rescuer also dies for three days and his followers lose all hope.)

The 'pass over.' One final plague remains, God tells Moses, before Pharoah expels the Israelites out of Egypt by royal decree. About midnight, God will pass through the land of Egypt, killing the firstborn of every animal and human in the kingdom. This horrible judgment is all-inclusive, from the firstborn of the king on his throne—the Pharoah's successor, whom Egyptian priests hailed as an incarnate god—to the lowliest slave-girl in the land.

Moses instructs the Israelites to kill a lamb for each household, to roast the meat, and to sprinkle some of the animal's blood down the sides and across the tops of their front doors. Each household is to eat a hasty meal comprised of the roasted lamb, accompanied by unleavened bread and bitter herbs. They are to eat with their traveling clothes on, with sandals on their feet, and with walking staffs in hand.

On this night God will see the lamb's blood on each door, and he will "pass over" those houses as he destroys the firstborn of all Egypt. The Israelites are to mark this event hereafter by making it the beginning month of their calendar. They also are to commemorate God's rescue from slavery by an annual Passover feast. In one house after another across Egypt, the firstborn child dies, and a wail goes up that echoes throughout the land. Pharoah finally orders the Hebrews to leave his land. They march out, their animals in tow, wearing Egyptian clothing and carrying Egyptian jewelry of all kinds.

Pharoah's finish. As the liberated Hebrews approach the Red Sea, Pharoah leads his army with 600 chariots in pursuit of the escaping slaves. God sends a great wind and divides the sea, and the Children of Israel march through on dry land. The Egyptians drive their chariots into the dry sea bed behind the fleeing Hebrews. God returns the waters to their normal state, drowning Pharoah and his pursuing army. The Israelites praise God and honor Moses.

Six

COVENANT MOUNTAIN

Not even Moses, who grew up in Pharoah's court, is prepared for the task he now faces. The people are no longer slaves, but, as they quickly realize, that is only half of the story. Accustomed to a predictable life, though often harsh, they now find themselves in an inhospitable and unknown wilderness. As their limited rations run out, they grumble and panic. Time after time, God provides for their needs.

Quail fly directly to the Israelites' camp and cover the ground. When the morning dew evaporates, it leaves as residue a mysterious flake-like substance that is both tasty and nutritious. The people call it "manna," Hebrew for "What is it?" The manna continues throughout their wilderness wanderings, then stops abruptly when they finally enter the Land of Canaan.

When the people complain of thirst, God tells Moses to strike a cliff with his shepherd's staff. Moses obeys and water flows from the rock, creating streams in the desert. When faced with attack by a marauding desert tribe known as the Amalekites, God empowers the Israelites' hastily-formed and untrained army, and the attackers flee in defeat.

The Majestic Mountain

The covenant announced. Less than 90 days after they leave
Egypt, the Israelites come to Mount Sinai, the same location
where God had appeared to Moses in the burning bush. God
instructs Moses to prepare the people for a divine encounter.
Through Moses, God tells the elders of the people:

> You yourselves have seen what I did to the Egyptians,
> and how I bore you on eagles' wings, and brought you
> to Myself. Now then, if you will indeed obey My voice
> and keep My covenant, then you shall be My own pos-
> session among all the peoples, for all the earth is Mine;
> and you shall be to Me a kingdom of priests and a holy
> nation.

The tribal leaders respond by promising to do everything
that Yahweh has commanded. Moses reports their response to
God. These Hebrews are a special people, made special by
God's choice and by his deliverance. Now they are about to
learn what that means, and the kind of life they are to live in
response to God's call and rescue.

For two days the people wait in anxious anticipation for their
invisible God to come. Then, on the third day, "the LORD came
down on Mount Sinai, to the top of the mountain." The rugged
mountain already struck awe into the people's hearts, accustomed as they were to the flatlands of Egypt. But now this
awesome scene turns foreboding. The mountain belches
smoke like a furnace. Tremors rumble through its cliffs and its
peaks begin to quake. A heavy cloud shrouds the sky until day
seems as night. Peals of thunder blast like a trumpet over the
mountain, echoing into the wilderness beyond. Flashes of lightning pierce the pitch-black sky. The God who rescues is no
domesticated deity. He is master of the primal elements, the
Creator of heaven and earth.

Then God speaks to the people. "I am the LORD your God," he announces, "who brought you out of the land of Egypt, out of the house of slavery. You shall have no other gods before Me." With this, God declares the Ten Commandments, the very core of all the Law of Moses. By this time, the people are so scared that they tremble. They approach Moses and beg that God not say any more, but instead speak to them through Moses. God agrees. The people stand at a distance while Moses approaches the thick cloud. God continues dictating the Law to Moses, regulating relationships of all kinds in this new society under God.

The covenant sealed. When God completes his instructions, Moses repeats them to the people. He then writes God's words in a Book of the Covenant, which he reads to the assembled people. The people formally promise to obey God's words. With these commitments, Moses sprinkles blood of young sacrificial bulls on the people, saying, "Behold, the blood of the covenant." The Great Rescuer will speak words much like these some day, but he will refer to his own blood and not that of slaughtered animals.

The Holy Sanctuary

The sacred tent. As the story continues, God gives Moses detailed, precise instructions for building a portable sanctuary called the Tabernacle. This sanctuary symbolizes God's presence among his covenant people, but its entire floor plan emphasizes the reality of their moral distance from God's pure holiness.

Enclosing this elaborate two-room structure is a courtyard surrounded by mounted curtains. Only the priests and their tribal-assistants, the Levites, may enter into this courtyard. A curtain or veil separates the outer room, called the Holy Place, from the interior room, known as the Most Holy Place or the Holy of Holies. That special room is off limits to all except the high priest himself.

In the courtyard stands a wooden altar for burning whole animals, constructed in such a way to catch the blood and to retain the ashes. Between the altar and the sanctuary entrance is a brass laver, or water basin, for ritual washings. The first compartment, the Holy Place, contains three items of sacred furniture: a lamp-stand or Menorah of pure gold, a gold-plated wooden table for the Bread of the Presence, and a golden altar for burning incense.

Inside the Most Holy Place is a gold-plated wooden chest called the Ark of the Covenant. Covering the ark is a lid of solid gold, known as the Mercy Seat. On the top of this lid stand two golden cherubim, a very high order of angels, whose wings spread upward toward the center of the Mercy Seat. Here the God who inhabits heaven will receive the sacrificial blood of animals as a covering for the people's guilt. This mysterious transaction will make more sense after many centuries have passed, when the Great Rescuer spreads his own arms and hangs between heaven and earth.

The priests. Sandwiched between those details, God instructs Moses to ordain his brother Aaron as high priest in Israel, and Aaron's sons and their descendants as priests. The priests represent the entire people before God, and the high priest represents them all.

The high priest's ceremonial clothing symbolizes the realities of the relationship between God and his ancient covenant people. On the high priest's turban is a gold plate with the inscription "Holy to the LORD." On his shoulder-pieces and on his breastplate are precious stones engraved with the names of the tribes of Israel. What this man does, he does on behalf of all Israel. When God accepts his sacrifices, God also accepts those whom he represents.

The high priest's chief duties occur on a single day each year—Yom Kippur, the Day of Atonement. On that day the high priest alone, hidden in a blanket of incense smoke, enters the Holy of Holies twice with sacrificial blood, first for himself and then for all the people. God takes note of the blood, which represents both innocent life and substitutionary death, and forgives the people's sins.

The high priest then exits the Tabernacle, to perform another ceremony symbolizing the reality of God's forgiveness. This time he lays his hands on a goat's head and confesses all the sins of the people, symbolically transferring those sins from the people to the animal. Someone then leads the goat out of the camp into the wilderness where it is abandoned. "And the goat shall bear on itself all their iniquities to a solitary land."

The divine presence. The Book of Exodus closes with the people building and furnishing the Tabernacle, and with God filling it with his presence. After Moses hangs the final curtain, we are told that "the cloud covered the tent of meeting, and the glory of the LORD filled the tabernacle. And Moses was not able to enter the tent of meeting because the cloud had settled on it, and the glory of the LORD filled the tabernacle."

God has saved his people out of Egypt and has bound himself to them by solemn covenant sealed with blood. The Tabernacle represents his presence. The priesthood represents his forgiveness. The people have promised to be faithful to the God who saved them. But if any Israelite who brought sacrifices to one of those priests at that Tabernacle ever supposed that these holy rituals guaranteed a happy and sunny future, he would have been sadly mistaken. It was not that God lacked the power to bless his people, or that he didn't love them enough to protect them from their enemies.

No, the problem was the same one we encountered with the first humans in the Garden of Eden—the people's own rebellious spirit and fickle will. They had bargained with God at the covenant mountain. According to that bargain, God's blessing depended on the people's loyalty to him. We are about to discover the treachery of human loyalty—and the weakness of a covenant with God that depends on such loyalty from fall-en sinners.

Seven

A CHECKERED HISTORY

Wilderness Wanderings

After two years in the wilderness of Sinai, the Children of Israel move northward into an area called Paran, just south of Canaan. There, at God's instruction, they select a representative from each tribe and send these 12 men into Canaan to spy out the land. After 40 days, the spies return with a unanimous report that the place is marvelously fruitful—"flowing with milk and honey." There are also fortified cities and occasional giants, and ten of the spies conclude that the Israelites cannot possibly take the land. Only Caleb and Joshua urge the people to move forward with confidence in God. The people ignore Caleb and Joshua and accept the majority report.

This unbelieving generation of adults will die in the wilderness, God tells Moses, where they will spend 40 years—one year for each day the spies were in the land. Joshua and Caleb, the two spies who trusted God's power, will survive the wilderness and enter the Promised Land. At this point, Moses gives a farewell address to the people (the Book of Deuteronomy). He concludes by reciting the blessings that await those who are faithful to God, and the plagues and punishments reserved for those who are not. Moses then views the Land of Canaan from a mountain top, appoints Joshua as his successor, and dies.

Into the Land

Under Joshua's leadership, the Israelites enter Canaan, spread through the countryside and overpower some fortified cities. Joshua apportions the entire territory among the 12 tribes; it will be their task actually to conquer the land with God's help. Joshua dies, and no one takes his place as leader over all of Israel.

This generation of Israelites has not personally experienced God's mighty deeds. Soon they are not only worshiping Yahweh but also the nature gods (Baals) and fertility deities (Astartes) of the pagan Canaanites. As punishment, various foreigners raid and plunder Israelite territory. Those attacked cry for God to help. God raises up tribal heroes (including one woman) called "judges," who rescue the people from the immediate threat. With time, the people stray again and the story repeats. This cycle continues through 15 judges, over a period of 200-300 years.

The United Kingdom

As the last judge Samuel (who also is a prophet) is growing old, the people ask for a king. Until now, God has been Israel's king. He has led, defended and provided for the Israelites—through individual men and women anointed with his own power and grace. The people's request for a king offends God, but he consents to give them what they have asked for.

Saul. At God's instruction, Samuel locates a man named Saul, from the small tribe of Benjamin. When Saul begins his reign, he is shy, even self-effacing, consciously dependent on God and ready to obey. As king, however, that humble spirit gradually disappears, and Saul becomes proud and independent of God. Eventually, the old prophet Samuel informs King Saul that God intends to replace him as king.

David. God then sends Samuel to the little village of Bethlehem, to the house of a man named Jesse from the tribe of Judah. There, Samuel anoints Jesse's youngest son, David, who until now has tended his father's sheep. God puts his Spirit on David, as he had done before with Saul. God also removes his Spirit from King Saul and sends an evil spirit to terrorize him.

David the shepherd boy takes provisions to his soldier brothers, who are in battle against the Philistines. There, he encounters Goliath, the blasphemous Philistine champion, who stands more than nine feet tall. David topples the giant with a stone from a sling and cuts off Goliath's head. David credits God for this victory, but the people credit David, who becomes a folk hero overnight. In King Saul's jealous mind, David also becomes a rival. From that point forward, Saul attempts to kill his presumed competitor.

Instead, Saul himself dies during a battle against the Philistines. David's clan of Judah proclaims him its tribal king, and David reigns in Hebron for seven-and-a-half years. Meanwhile, Saul's military loyalists recognize Saul's son Ishbosheth as king and civil war ensues. Ishbosheth is assassinated by his own officers, however, and all the tribes accept David as Israel's uncontested king. In a move of brilliant political strategy, David conquers the Jebusite city of Jerusalem, which had no previous history within any Israelite tribe, and makes it his independent capital.

David then locates the Ark of the Covenant, which for 20 years had sat in a private home after being returned from Philistine capture. He brings the Ark to Jerusalem, now called the City of David, and places it in a tent. After a while, David decides to build a permanent temple for the Ark of the Covenant, and tells the prophet Nathan his desire. God reminds David, through Nathan, that a tent was God's original choice for the Ark. God honors David's good intentions, however, and promises to build him a "house"—a family dynasty—and to give to one of David's descendants a throne that will endure forever.

David's story is the story of a faithful man of God, who at times failed miserably and sinned greatly, but who also repented genuinely. It is the story of divine strength and human weakness, of earthly crisis and heavenly rescue. It is the story of God working through human circumstances and choices and conduct—often times in spite of those things—to deliver his people and to accomplish his saving purpose.

Solomon. Before David dies, he arranges the coronation of his son Solomon as his successor. Shortly after David's death, God appears to Solomon in a dream and offers him anything he might ask. Humble in the face of his new responsibilities, Solomon requests "an understanding heart to discern between good and evil." God grants his request. Additionally, because Solomon had not selfishly asked for long life, riches and honor, God gives him those things as well.

Solomon's wisdom becomes legendary throughout the ancient world. Solomon also negotiates treaties far and wide, and accumulates a harem of 700 wives. His merchant ships sail the Mediterranean world and beyond. Riches of every description pour into Jerusalem, until silver becomes as common as rocks. Solomon's greatest achievement, however, is certainly his building of the Temple of God. A truly magnificent structure, the Temple consists of enormous stones, which workmen shape in advance and assemble like a giant jigsaw puzzle. As in the ancient Tabernacle, the holy furniture is largely made of gold.

As the Bible story continues, Solomon dedicates the finished Temple with solemn ceremony. The priests bring in the Ark of the Covenant, and the glory-cloud of God fills the Temple. This sanctuary symbolizes God's Presence, Solomon acknowledges, although God made the universe and cannot possibly be contained in any building made by man.

Together, people and king reaffirm their allegiance to God.

God accepts this dedication and promises to bless Solomon and his heirs so long as they remain faithful to him. However, if they forsake God, he warns, this Temple will do them no good. God will remove the people from their land, and the Temple itself will become a heap of ruins.

Unfortunately, Solomon's building projects do not stop with Yahweh's Temple—he also builds shrines for the pagan deities of his many foreign wives. By doing this, the king flagrantly rebels against the covenant-God of Israel. For this evil, God tells Solomon, he will remove the kingdom from Solomon's family and give it to a servant. For David's sake, however, he will do this after Solomon dies. Also for the sake of David and for Jerusalem, God will leave one tribe in the hands of Solomon's royal heirs.

The Divided Kingdoms

Solomon dies and his son Rehoboam succeeds him on the throne. Rehoboam foolishly oppresses the people, taxes them heavily, and makes them slaves of the state. The people rebel, and all the tribes except Judah and little Benjamin reject Solomon's son as king. Instead they choose Jereboam, a servant of Solomon. So, about 922 B.C., the united kingdom divides into two competing and often-warring kingdoms of Judah (in the South) and of Israel (in the North).

To minimize competing loyalties associated with Jeru-salem, Jereboam erects two golden bulls at strategic ancient sites within his own northern kingdom and proclaims these as shrines of the gods who brought Israel's ancestors out of Egypt. He also institutes a rival priesthood, not from the tribe of Levi, and substitutes a religious calendar different from the holy days established through Moses. By these rebellious acts against Yahweh, Jereboam earns the description that follows him throughout the rest of the Old Testament—"Jereboam, the son of Nebat, who caused Israel to sin."

The two kingdoms contrast sharply, in outer stability and in inner character. Throughout its 200 years, the northern kingdom of Israel sees frequent assassinations and palace coups. Only two of its many royal families, those of Omri (about 880 B.C.) and Jehu (about 841 B.C.) endure more than two generations. In Jerusalem, on the other hand, David's royal descendants reign for more than 325 years without interruption.

In general, the kings of Israel ignore God's laws and covenant. The kings of Judah alternate between good and evil. During much of their history, both kingdoms are at war—with regional neighbors, with world powers such as Egypt, Assyria and Babylon, and sometimes with each other.

Kingdoms into Exile

Israel to Assyria. Both kingdoms enjoy a period of peaceful prosperity during the mid-8th century B.C., but material well-being is offset by spiritual indifference. These decades on either side of 740 B.C. are times of great prophetic preaching—of Isaiah and Micah in Judah, and Amos and Hosea in Israel. The northern kingdom ignores God's call to repentance. In 721 B.C., the Assyrian king Sargon overthrows the national capital of Samaria and carries the population away into Assyria (today's Iraq). Nine years later, the newly-risen forces of Babylon (also today's Iraq) capture the Assyrian capital Nineveh and become the major power.

Judah to Babylon. Meanwhile, King Hezekiah leads the southern kingdom in spiritual revival, and God spares that kingdom for another 125 years. By then, however, the kingdom of Judah also forsakes God. His patience exhausted, God allows Nebuchadnezzar to conquer Jerusalem, destroy the Temple and take the people, as captives, to Babylon (601-582 B.C.).

This is also a time of great prophets. Jeremiah laments Jerusalem's doom and predicts the people's return. Ezekiel and Daniel both go into Babylonian Captivity. Ezekiel prophesies among the captives; Daniel serves in the court of the king.

Return to the Homeland

The decree of Cyrus. About 539 B.C., Cyrus, king of Persia (today's Iran), conquers Babylon. The following year, Cyrus issues decrees allowing captives to return to their homelands, including the people of Judah, as Isaiah had prophesied two centuries before. The Jews return in several waves.

The next year, a large group returns with Zerubbabel to rebuild the Temple. The prophets Haggai and Zechariah encourage this endeavor. In 516 B.C., the Temple is completed—on a scale far less grand than Solomon's original. Sixty years later, Ezra leads another group to the homeland. Nehemiah goes to Jerusalem, perhaps 12 years after Ezra's return, and rebuilds the protective city wall.

Malachi's final word. By the time of Malachi, somewhere between 460-400 B.C., Israel has fallen into religious carelessness and spiritual indifference. Even after all of God's mighty rescues through the centuries, his people are ignoring him again. Malachi rebukes them sternly with a series of rhetorical questions. He predicts a day when God will reduce evildoers to ashes and make his faithful people rejoice.

But before these climactic events, God will send his messenger, code-named "Elijah the prophet," and the Lord himself will "come suddenly to his temple." Once more—this time decisively and for all eternity—God himself will accomplish the necessary saving deed. With this, the Old Testament Scriptures end. Four hundred years go by before the New Testament Gospels continue the sacred Story.

Eight

PREVIEWS OF THE RESCUER

God's victory over sin, and his Great Rescue of sinners from its power and effects, is certainly the most significant accomplishment in human history. It ought not to surprise us, therefore, that God began announcing those coming events from earliest times. God regularly announces great deeds before he performs them. We see this throughout the entire Old Testament story.

God Declares, Saves, Proclaims

The principle stated. Moses stated the principle to Israel in its infancy, as they were about to cross the Jordan River into the Promised Land. When God wants you to know the future, Moses explained, he will send you a prophet. This means that witches, sorcerers, soothsayers and the like are off limits. If a prophet is truly from God, his prophecy will come to pass. If the message proves to be false, he is not from God. (Deut. 18:18-22.)

God later repeated the principle through Amos. "Surely the LORD God does nothing," Amos said, "unless he reveals his secret counsel to his servants the prophets" (Amos 3:7). Perhaps the clearest statement, however, comes through Isaiah, Amos' contemporary in the south. Yahweh reveals himself in three stages, he told Isaiah, and his revelation involves both word and deed:

> I, even I, am the LORD;
> And there is no savior besides Me.
> It is I who have declared and saved and proclaimed
> (Isa. 43:11-12).

God fearlessly declares what he intends to do—then he accomplishes his saving deed—then he proclaims what he has done. No other god has ever done this, Isaiah points out. Only Yahweh dares to announce his plans in advance, because he alone is sovereign and has the power to accomplish whatever he intends and predicts.

The principle illustrated. We see this pattern demonstrated throughout Israel's history. Centuries before the Exodus, God declared to childless Abram that his descendants would eventually be slaves in a foreign land, but that God would judge their captors and bring them out with great possessions (Gen. 15:12-14). Generations later, God saved the Israelites from Egyptian bondage, just as he had declared. Then, at Mount Sinai, God proclaimed himself to Israel as the God who had saved them, and told them what he expected in return.

The same three-part revelation occurs also near the other end of Old Testament history, when God again delivers his people from national captivity—this time in Babylon. God declared that he would send the people of Judah into Babylon for 70 years as punishment for their sins, and that he would then bring them home again through a king named Cyrus (Jer. 25:8-12; Isa. 44:24-45:7; Dan. 9:1-3). Generations later, God saved the Jews from Babylon, just as he had declared. Then, through the prophets Haggai, Zechariah and Malachi, God proclaimed to the returnees how he had saved them, and told them what he expected in return.

General Announcements of Jesus Christ

When we come to God's deliverance through the Great Rescuer, we find the same three-fold pattern. Throughout Old Testament history from Adam to Malachi, God declared his intention to rescue from sin and all its results. The Gospels of Matthew, Mark, Luke and John in the New Testament tell exactly how God saved sinners, just as he had declared. In the Book of Acts and the New Testament Epistles, God proclaimed the salvation he accomplished through Jesus, and instructed rescued sinners how to respond to his great deliverance.

Eve's descendant. God first announced the Great Rescue to Adam and Eve after they sinned in the Garden of Eden. In pronouncing sentence on the serpent (Satan), God said: "I will put enmity between you and the woman, and between your seed and her seed; He shall bruise you on the head, and you shall bruise him on the heel" (Gen. 3:15).

Bearing out this prophecy, the Gospels record the lifelong conflict between Satan and Jesus, Eve's ultimate descendant in this prophecy. The Book of Revelation portrays the cosmic struggle in powerful, dramatic symbols drawn from ancient Genesis. Satan constantly nips at Jesus' heel, as it were, but Jesus finally crushes Satan's head with a fatal blow. As believers in Jesus, we share in this same victory, which some day will become visible to all (Rom. 16:19-20).

Abram's offspring. When God called Abram from Ur in Chaldea, he promised the patriarch a package of blessings. As one part of the promise, God told Abram: "in you all the families of the earth shall be blessed" (Gen. 12:3). Centuries later, Paul quotes this passage from Genesis, which he says was "foreseeing that God would justify the Gentiles by faith." By making this promise, God "preached the gospel beforehand to Abraham" (Gal. 3:8-9). Jesus himself once told some fellow Jews, "your father Abraham rejoiced to see My day; and he saw it, and was glad" (John 8:56).

Judah's lineage. When Abraham's grandson Jacob was dying, he pronounced inspired blessings on each of his 12 sons. Judah's lineage, predicted old Jacob, would enjoy royal status, possessing the "scepter" and "the ruler's staff." From Judah's kingly line would finally come one whom Jacob calls "Shiloh"—a word which may also be translated as "he to whom it belongs." This one would receive "the obedience of the peoples." (Gen. 49:10.) This "Shiloh" is Jesus Christ himself, a descendant of Judah, whom God has given authority over all the peoples of the world (Matt. 1:1-3; 28:18-20).

Star and scepter. A very similar prophecy occurs in the oracle of Balaam, a foreign prophet whom the king of Moab hired to place a curse on the Israelites as they approached the Land of Canaan. The Bible does not say whether Balaam spoke for Yahweh at other times, but it says that God took charge of his mouth on this occasion. Each time that Balaam tried to curse the Israelites, he pronounced a blessing on them instead.

Finally, Balaam's prophecy moves beyond the people in general to focus on an individual in the distant future. "I see him," spoke Balaam, "but not near; a star shall come forth from Jacob, and a scepter shall rise from Israel." Then he adds: "One from Jacob shall have dominion" (Num. 24:17, 19). This text suddenly becomes meaningful when we read about the star at Jesus' birth, the Savior born to reign over Israel and the nations.

A prophet like Moses. We have already quoted God's promise to speak to Israel through prophets (Deut. 18:15). This promise included all the prophets sent by God, but its greatest fulfillment is Jesus Christ himself (Acts 3:18, 22-26). As the Epistle to the Hebrews explains, Jesus is God's greatest Prophet to humankind, because he reveals God's very character and nature in a human life (Heb. 1:1-4).

A daring leader. Centuries after Moses, near the beginning of the Babylonian Captivity, Jeremiah prophesied of a coming ruler who would spring up from among the people, but who would stand in God's presence on their behalf. "Their leader shall be one of them," the prophet announced, "and their ruler shall come forth from their midst. And I will bring him near, and he shall approach Me; for who would dare to risk his life to approach Me? declares the LORD" (Jer. 30:21).

Symbols and Metaphors of Jesus

The Old Testament is filled with people, sacred objects and significant events that, viewed later in light of Jesus, seem to foreshadow his person, his deeds and the results of his work. New Testament writers call attention to some of these symbols and metaphors. Later Christian authors have noted even more.

People. We might think of Adam, the head of the human race, who acted (although for bad, not for good) as a representative of all his descendants. There is Noah, who, like Jesus, symbolized the transition from an old world to a world washed fresh and clean. Melchizedek, the king-priest of ancient Jerusalem, prefigured the priesthood of Jesus, which is based on his personal character and endures forever, rather than resting on physical qualifications with term limits.

Isaac provides a preview of Jesus who, like himself, was his father's beloved son and carried the wood for his own death. Joseph not only shared a name with Jesus' stepfather many centuries later, but both men had dreams, both were morally virtuous and both saved their families by taking them to Egypt.

Events. Moses' birth and Jesus' birth involved many elements in common. Both stories included a wicked king who decreed the murder of innocent children. Both featured a baby spared, through whom God delivered his people. Both stories told of wise men on whom the king relied. Both included a special light at the baby's birth (in Jewish tradition, in Moses' case). Both involved a flight by night to escape the evil king.

The original Passover event foreshadowed Jesus, by whose blood his people escape divine judgment. Jesus also fulfilled the Exodus story. Just as Israel came out of Egypt, crossed the water, entered the desert and went to a mountain to receive God's law, so Matthew shows Jesus returning from Egypt, going to the Jordan for baptism, being tempted in the desert, then going up on a mountain to explain the true meaning of God's law.

Sacred things. The rock that provided Israel with water in the wilderness prefigured Jesus Christ, the living water who nourishes those who trust in him. The Levitical priesthood pointed to Jesus, in its meaning (a "clean" life offered as a substitute for the life of the guilty person) and in the significance of the high-priestly vestments (a man who satisfies the demands of God's holiness, while representing his people who are sinners). So did the sacrificial system, especially the sin offerings, and—if some Christian interpreters are correct —even the furniture in the Tabernacle. Jesus is "Joshua" in Hebrew, who, like Moses' successor of that name, led God's people into a land of promise.

Jesus is the true Tabernacle and Temple, in whom God was present among humans. God's "glory," which filled both those Old Testament sanctuaries, shines out from Jesus—on the Mount of Transfiguration in some Gospels and through his miraculous "signs" in the Gospel of John. Jesus is the fulfillment of God's promise to establish David's dynasty forever. These are only samples of such metaphors and symbols—the person who reads the Old Testament with Jesus in mind can discover very many more.

Specific Prophecies of the Savior

The Old Testament also contains many very specific prophecies concerning the birth, ministry, death, resurrection and ascension of Jesus Christ—as well as the divine kingdom of universal peace and blessing that he will bring to reality at his yet-future return. Some of these prophecies had an immediate limited meaning in their original context, with a deeper and richer fulfillment in Jesus Christ. Others had no apparent fulfillment when first spoken, but became crystal clear after Jesus had fulfilled them. Indeed, the prophets themselves sometimes asked God the meaning of their own prophecies, but God revealed to them that the fulfillments were for a future time (1 Pet. 1:10-12).

That said, these ancient prophecies were "concealed and sealed up until the end time" (Dan. 12:8-9). After the "end time" began—with Jesus' resurrection and the coming of the Holy Spirit—"those who have insight" through the gospel will understand (Dan. 12:8-10). Taken together, and especially with Christian hindsight, these prophecies present a rather detailed picture of the story of Jesus Christ.

Jesus Fulfills the Prophecies

In his birth. The Savior appears, not with fanfare and public excitement, but like a root out of a parched ground (Isa. 53:2). He comes as a human being, to do the perfect will of God (Psalm 40:6-8; Heb. 10:4-10). He does not suddenly appear as a mighty hero; he is born as a tiny baby (Isa. 9:6-8). Indeed, what a birth! A virgin conceives and bears this son (Isa. 7:14, Greek.; Matt. 1:22-23). This birth occurs in Bethlehem of Judea (Micah 5:2-5; Matt. 2:5-6).

This baby is fully human—he is no angel or demigod of pagan legend. But he is also begotten by the Spirit of God, the divine son who will rule the nations with a rod of iron (Psalm 2:7-9; Matt. 3:17; Rev. 12:5). After his birth in Bethlehem, he goes to Egypt and comes out again (Hosea 11:1; Matt. 2:16). During his infancy we hear mothers weeping; their babies have been killed (Jer. 31:15; Matt. 2:17-18).

In his ministry. When the time comes for his public ministry, a voice cries out in the wilderness, "Prepare a road for the LORD" (Isa. 40:3-6; Lk. 3:4-6). When Jesus is baptized, God tears the heavens open and comes down to save (Isa. 54:1;

Mark 1:10). He anoints Jesus with his own Spirit (Isa. 61:1-2; Lk. 4:16-21). The Savior's ministry begins in Galilee, near the Sea of that name (Isa. 9:1-2; Matt. 4:13-17).

Each new day Jesus listens to God and does exactly what God tells him (Isa. 50:4-6; John 5:19-20). He heals the people, taking their weaknesses and diseases on himself (Isa. 53:4; Matt. 8:16-17). He opens blind eyes, unstops deaf ears and enables lame legs to leap like a deer (Isa. 35:5-6; Matt. 11:3-6). Because of him, some families split apart (Micah 7:6; Matt. 10:34-36). Yet his ministry is not flamboyant; he quietly brings about justice (Isa. 42:1-4; Matt. 12:15-21). He teaches in parables to hide the truth from the insincere (Isa. 6:9-10; Matt. 13:13-15).

In his death. One day this gentle king rides into Jerusalem on a lowly donkey (Zech. 9:9; Matt. 21:1-5). There he chases the thieves out of God's house, restoring it as a house of prayer (Isa. 56:7; Jer. 7:11; Matt. 21:12-13). He is consumed with zeal for God (Psalm 69:9; John 2:17). Although he is God's chosen one, the Messiah's own people reject him (Psalm 118:22-23; John 1:11). Someone sells him for 30 pieces of silver—then uses the money to buy a potter's depleted field (Zech. 11:12; Matt. 27:6-10).

His enemies beat this spiritual Shepherd and his "sheep" all scatter (Zech. 13:7; Matt. 26:31). His enemies pierce him (Zech. 12:10; John 19:37). He is beaten, bruised and put to death for the sins of others. Throughout it all he remains as silent and defenseless as a lamb going to slaughter. Taking the wrongs of others into his own person, he sets sinners right with God (Isa. 53:5-8; 1 Pet. 2:21). In the process, he himself is forsaken by God (Psalm 22:1-2; Matt. 27:46). Yet he entrusts himself to God with his dying breath (Psalm 22:9-11; Lk. 23:46).

In resurrection and glory. Although put to death, the Savior does not remain dead, for God brings him back to life (Psalm 16:7-11; Acts 2:31-32). He ascends in the clouds to heaven itself (Psalm 24:7-10; Acts 1:9-11). There, God crowns him with authority, glory and an everlasting kingdom that will include people from every nation (Dan. 7:13-14).

Jesus, who willingly becomes lower than angels in becoming human, now is exalted far above angels; one day his people will occupy the glorious position that God originally created human beings to enjoy (Psalm 8:4-8; Heb. 2:5-10). Jesus takes his place at God's right side, waiting until all his enemies bow before his feet (Psalm 110:1; Acts 2:34; 1 Cor. 15:25).

There he intercedes for his people, divinely appointed to be their priest forever (Psalm 110:4; Heb. 7). God saves all who call on his name, and pours out the Holy Spirit on all his people (Joel 2:28-32; Acts 2:16-21). A new covenant unites God and his people—a covenant that depends on God's ability and not on the power of the people (Jer. 31:31-34; Heb. 8:6-13).

Still More to Come

Waiting until. All this has happened already to Jesus of Nazareth, the descendant of Eve, Abram, Judah and David. Every one of these details finds its place in the story of his birth, his ministry and life, his death and resurrection, his ascension and exaltation in heaven, his sending the Holy Spirit to his people.

But Jesus will not remain forever in heaven. He is there until—"until the period of restoration of all things, about which God spoke by the mouth of His holy prophets from ancient time" (Acts 3:18-21). God already has fulfilled his promises concerning the suffering of Christ, but he has not yet fulfilled all that he said concerning the glories to follow (1 Pet. 1:11).

About these matters, the ancient prophets said much indeed. They looked for a time when God would "destroy the power of the kingdoms of the nations" and God's rule would replace human rule (Haggai 2:22). The result will be universal peace; all creation will enjoy perfect harmony. Then "the earth will be full of the knowledge of the LORD as the waters cover the sea" (Isa. 11:4-9).

God will destroy death forever and wipe away his people's tears (Isa. 25:7-8). His name will be great among the nations; the whole earth will worship God (Mal. 1:11). God will live forever among his people in a covenant of peace (Ezek. 37:24-28). Everything will be holy, for evil will be gone; nothing will separate or hide God from his people (Zech. 14:20-21).

But we are getting ahead of ourselves. For none of that would ever happen, none could ever happen, apart from the Great Rescue. And that central deed, we are about to discover, involved a series of events so astounding that even the angels in heaven were surprised.

Nine

THE GOD-MAN

The ancient prophecies predict two truths that seem at first to clash. On the one hand, the prophets declare that God himself is the Savior who will personally rescue his people from sin and its effects. On the other hand, many prophecies identify the Great Rescuer as a descendant of Eve, of Abraham, of Jacob and Judah and David. The solution to this apparent contradiction lies in an amazing truth, about which the Old Testament contains only hints and clues.

A Savior Human and Divine

Ancient clues. The amazing truth is that the Great Rescuer is both human and divine—the God-man Jesus of Nazareth. Isaiah had hinted at this dual nature when, speaking of the Messiah, he promised: "For a child will be born to us, a son will be given to us" (Isa. 9:6).

The Savior will be a human baby, but he will be given—as though he existed before he was born or even conceived. Isaiah continued: "His name will be called ... Mighty God, Eternal Father, Prince of Peace"—identifying him with God himself (Isa. 9:6). Yet he will govern in righteousness and in peace "on the throne of David and over his kingdom" forever (Isa. 9:7). This Savior will be David's descendant, fully human (2 Sam. 7:12). Yet, as David himself prophesied, this descendant of David will also be David's "Lord" (Ps. 110:1).

How can this be? How can both promises be true? The answer comes in the bold conclusion of Isaiah's prophecy. "The zeal of the LORD of hosts will accomplish this" (Isa. 9:7). This promise brings us full circle to the place where we began. God himself will save his people from their sin. The authors of the New Testament consistently repeat this truth, although they express it in a variety of ways.

A virgin mother. Approximately six and seven centuries after Jeremiah and Isaiah, respectively, God comes as he had promised, in the birth of Jesus of Nazareth. Jesus is divinely born to a virgin mother, to whom a heavenly angel appears in advance and obtains her consent. An angel also appears to the virgin's betrothed, explaining her miraculous conception and quieting his fears that she has been unfaithful to him.

Luke's Gospel tells the story of young Mary, engaged to a man named Joseph. He is a descendant of David and so, it appears, is she. One day as Mary goes about her business, an angel suddenly appears and identifies himself as Gabriel (Lk. 1:26-27). Mary's shocked reaction was no doubt heightened if she remembered this name "Gabriel." This was the very same angel who had appeared to the prophet Daniel hundreds of years before, revealing to him the time of the Savior's future coming and describing the effects of the mighty rescue operation he would perform (Dan. 9:20-27).

"You have found favor with God," Gabriel tells Mary. "You will conceive in your womb, and bear a son, and you shall name Him Jesus. He will be great, and will be called the Son of the Most High; and the Lord God will give Him the throne of His father David; and He will reign over the house of Jacob forever; and His kingdom will have no end" (Lk. 1:30-33). The

Old Testament prophecies come tumbling together in this angelic announcement! How Mary's heart must have fluttered, even as her spirit soared! But "how," she also asks, "can this be, since I am a virgin?" (Lk. 1:34).

Gabriel gently answers. "The Holy Spirit will come upon you," he said, "and the power of the Most High will overshadow you; and for that reason the holy offspring shall be called the Son of God" (Lk. 1:35). The son of Mary is also the Son of God. The descendant of Eve is, in some mysterious sense, Eve's Creator. The baby Jesus is both human and divine. To Mary, it seems impossible. But Gabriel's final answer echoes the conclusion of Isaiah's prophecy about the baby who will be both God and man. "Nothing will be impossible with God" (Lk. 1:37).

Confronted with such an announcement, Mary responds in self-surrender and total trust. "Behold, the bond slave of the Lord," she replies to Gabriel. "Be it done to me according to your word" (v. 38). So the virgin Mary becomes pregnant. But, whether through fear or through faith, she does not tell any of this to Joseph, her espoused husband-to-be. Joseph will learn these wondrous details from his own angelic visitation.

But before Joseph hears from an angel, he discovers that his future wife is already pregnant (Matt. 1:18). Joseph knows that Mary has not had sex with him, but that is all he knows. If she is carrying some other man's baby, under Jewish law she is an adulteress. At the least, if this is true, she has shamed Joseph and destroyed all hopes of becoming his wife. At worst, she has committed a capital offense and faces the danger of death by stoning.

Joseph considers the possibilities and weighs his options. Finally he reaches his decision. He will break off the engagement quietly—more like a divorce according to Jewish custom—but he will never humiliate his Mary by exposing her to public disdain. (Matt. 1:19.)

Settled on this solution to a most embarrassing situation, Joseph goes to sleep one night, never anticipating the astounding announcement he is about to hear. As he sleeps, he dreams, and in his dream an angel of God appears and speaks with him face to face. "Joseph, son of David, do not be afraid to take Mary as your wife; for that which has been conceived in her is of the Holy Spirit. And she will bear a Son, and you shall call His name Jesus, for it is He who will save His people from their sins" (Matt. 1:20-21).

Every mother likely imagines her baby's future. Most fathers daydream about their children growing up. But no parent could have imagined the destiny of Mary's baby boy. Only God knew all that this son would accomplish. Baby Jesus was the long-awaited Savior, Israel's Messiah, the redeemer of the world. He was born for a singular purpose: to save God's people—Jews and Gentiles alike—from their sins.

Isaiah's prophecy had finally come to pass. A Jewish maiden gave birth to a baby son. But this son of a virgin mother was more than Mary's son. He was also "Immanuel," Hebrew for "God with us" (Matt. 1:22-23; Isa. 7:14).

A heavenly affirmation. Mark's Gospel does not contain a nativity story. It does not include the angelic visitations to Mary or to Joseph. It simply begins with the introduction: "The beginning of the gospel of Jesus Christ, the Son of God" (Mark 1:1). Immediately following that introduction, Mark quotes prophecies from Malachi and from Isaiah concerning someone who will announce God's own appearance and prepare a route for his arrival (Mark 1:2-3).

This man who announces the coming of Jesus is John the Baptist (Mark 1:4-8). Jesus comes to John for baptism, and God confirms his divine and messianic identity three separate ways: the heavens part, God's Spirit descends upon Jesus, and a voice from heaven acknowledges Jesus as God's Son (Mark 1:9-11). Each aspect fulfills a specific Old Testament prophecy.

"O that You would rend the heavens and come down," Isaiah had pleaded with God (Isa. 65:1). How the prophet longed for God to come and save his people! "All of us have become like one who is unclean," Isaiah lamented, "and all our righteous deeds are like a filthy garment" (Isa. 65:6). When will God come and rescue his people from their sin?

Other Gospels report the heavens opening at Jesus' baptism, but Mark alone literally says that the heavens were "torn" open. God had answered Isaiah's prayer by coming in the person of Jesus. Mark uses this same Greek word for "torn" at Jesus' death, to describe the spontaneous tearing of the Temple curtain that separated the outer sanctuary from the Holy of Holies (Mark 15:38). This event signifies in a dramatic way that through Jesus' life and death God has finally removed the barrier that stood between himself and his people (Heb. 10:19-20).

The Spirit descends on Jesus, fulfilling the second preview of the Messiah contained in Isaiah. In Isaiah's prophetic vision, the Messiah declares: "The Spirit of the Lord GOD is upon me, because the LORD has anointed me—to bring good news to the afflicted; He has sent me to bind up the brokenhearted, to proclaim liberty to captives, and freedom to prisoners; to proclaim the favorable year of the LORD, and the day of vengeance of our God" (Isa. 61:1-2). This is the meaning of the title "Messiah" or "Christ"—the Anointed One—anointed, confirmed, empowered with the very Spirit of Yahweh himself.

As third confirmation, a voice comes out of the heavens: "You are My beloved Son, with You I am well pleased" (Mark 1:11). This statement is packed with meaning for every Jew familiar with the Old Testament. God calls the Messiah his "son" in Psalm 2:7. Isaiah foretells the coming of God's chosen Servant, in whom the Almighty delights and on whom he places his Spirit (Isa. 42:1).

God's embodied Presence. John's Gospel also affirms that in Jesus of Nazareth, God himself came to earth and saved sinners, but he phrases the truth in terms of Greek philosophy. God's Logos ("Word" or "Reason") has always existed. When

God spoke and created the universe, his Word was personal. It was with God and it was divine (John 1:1-3).

This divine and personal Word became flesh in the man Jesus of Nazareth and "tabernacled" among us—imagery clearly borrowed from the Old Testament. Just as God once resided among his people in the Tabernacle and later the Temple, now he resided with them in the person of the man Jesus Christ. "We beheld His glory," John continues—bringing to mind the glory-cloud that filled God's ancient sanctuaries and symbolized his presence—"glory as of the only begotten from the Father, full of grace and truth" (v. 14).

Throughout the Gospel of John, the divine "glory" becomes more and more transparent, shining as it were through the flesh of Jesus. As Jesus performs his miracles, which John calls "signs" (because they signified his true identity), his "glory" shines more and more brightly (John 2:11).

God's fullness in human flesh. The author of Hebrews tells us that the man Jesus, whom we know as God's Son, is actually the one through whom God made the worlds. He is "the radiance" of God's "glory" and "the exact representation of His nature" (Heb. 1:1-3).

The Apostle Paul borrowed language of his time to preach this same sermon. "God was in Christ reconciling the world to Himself" (2 Cor. 5:19). Jesus "is the image of the invisible God" (Col. 1:15). "All things were created" through Jesus and for Jesus (Col. 1:16). Jesus existed "before all things" and holds all things together (Col. 1:17). In the man Jesus, God reconciled all things to Himself (Col. 1:20). In Jesus, "all the fullness of Deity dwells in bodily form" (Col. 2:9).

The bigger miracle. By becoming a man, Paul reminds us, Jesus exchanged riches for poverty—to make us poor sinners rich (2 Cor. 8:9). Jesus "existed in the form of God" but "emptied" himself to be "made in the likeness of men" (Phil. 2:5-7). Although New Testament writers outside the Gospels do not mention Mary's virginal conception, they repeatedly affirm the truth behind those mechanics—that God himself came to earth in Jesus Christ to rescue sinners.

That is the greatest miracle of this story. In Jesus, the God of the Old Testament fulfills his ancient promises and prophecies. Jesus is Israel's Messiah and the Savior of humankind, but he is more. He is Immanuel—"God with us." Equally amazing, Jesus is also man. Not just a man—not merely any man. He is *the* man, like Adam in the beginning, a new humankind in one human being. Jesus is not only God with us, he is also the Last Adam.

Ten

A NEW ADAM

A Foolproof Arrangement

The need. If human history had made anything clear, it was surely this—sinful men and women could never save themselves. Equally obvious from Heaven's perspective, every descendant of Adam fell within the "sinful" category—all of them by nature, and every responsible adult by personal choice. If God was ever to rescue his fallen and rebellious human creatures from the clutch and the consequences of sin, he must devise a method that did not depend on their success—either in making right decisions or in carrying them out.

Adam had proved the necessity for that and Israel had removed any remaining doubt. What was needed, as God had whispered through Jeremiah centuries before, was a whole new arrangement—a new covenant—a new relationship based on something better and more solid than the performance of the very sinners who so desperately needed divine intervention. God would have to do this job for himself.

God's eternal plan. It was not that God gradually realized the problem, or that he suddenly stumbled upon the solution. He had known it all from the beginning, before he made humans or even the universe itself. He had seen it coming—the

Creation, the Garden, the Man's wrongheadedness and rebellious heart. God anticipated the alienation from himself, the loss of the Tree of Life, the ever-increasing power of sin and all its destructive consequences.

But the Almighty also saw more. He saw another Man who would be more than man. He would be God himself. This Man would think correctly, binding his will to the wishes of God's own heart. He would make right choices—also in a Garden. He, too, would become separated from God, but only briefly. Then he would conquer death, break the bonds of sin and release a greater power. And eventually—when the clock of this universe was ready to tick its last, this Man would usher in a new creation and restore the Tree of Life.

The substitute. This, then, was the solution: God himself came to earth in the man Jesus of Nazareth, as the personal representative of every human who finally would be saved. He took the place of them all—living for them, dying for them, establishing a record with his own life by which they would then be judged. What the Creator had always desired from the human creature, Jesus provided on their behalf. God counted Jesus' own accomplishments as theirs: his faithful commitment to the Father, his daily choices, his consistent obedience.

When he had lived a perfect life for the Father, Jesus personally accepted the punishment for his people's wrongs. God counted his suffering as theirs: the pain of being betrayed, the stripes of the whip on his back, the spit on his cheeks, the nails in his hands, his unanswered cry to the Father above. Finally, God accepted Jesus' death itself on behalf of all he would save—the death weighted down by guilt not his own, the death demanded of sinners, the death prescribed by the curses of a broken covenant, the death first announced in Eden, the death on that middle cross on Golgotha on the darkest day in human history.

By his own perfect doing and his own perfect dying, by his actions and his passions, by all that he did and all that was done to him, Jesus removed forever the sin that separated God and his people. In its place, forever approved by his resurrection and sealed by his presence in heaven, Jesus gave God a human life of total commitment, the perfect obedience of a loving and trusting heart, the very gift that God wanted from Adam and Eve and from all his human creatures but had never received.

Jesus the Last Adam

When God made Adam and Eve and placed them in Paradise, the arrangement was simple and straightforward. Although they were God's creatures and totally dependent on him for existence, they were made in his image for fellowship with the Creator himself. His new world was now theirs to enjoy with him. All they had to do was to trust him as God and do what he said. Obedience would bring life. Disobedience would bring death. "Don't eat the tree in the middle of the Garden," God told them plainly. So that is exactly what they proceeded to do. We have already seen the dire results of that rebellion for all of Adam's descendants.

Adam the First. Jesus comes as the Last Adam (there are only two such representatives in the human race; each appears at the beginning of a new creation). He retraces Adam's steps, as it were, stepping correctly at every point where Adam slipped. Jesus does right all that Adam did wrong. To appreciate the contrast between these two representative men, we need to pause for a moment and remember the path that Adam followed.

Adam was made in God's image. Not content with that, he grasped for more. He wanted equality with God himself; he coveted God's right to say what is good and what is evil. Although he was only a man, Adam grabbed for the prize that was not rightly his. Motivated by personal ambition, he left off creaturely humility and disobeyed God's single prohibition. As a result of his prideful disobedience, Adam died—and brought under the power of Death all those whom he represented.

Adam the Second.   But then came Jesus, the second and Last Adam. The Gospel writer Luke hints at this truth in giving the genealogy of Jesus. Unlike Matthew, who opens his gospel with Jesus' family tree, Luke (who traces a slightly different line) places the ancestral list just after the baptism of Jesus by John. As Jesus emerges from the Jordan, God speaks from heaven: "You are My beloved Son," he tells the Savior (Lk. 3:22). Jesus' neighbors, however, supposed that he was Joseph's son (v. 23). In actual fact, Luke continues, Jesus genealogy goes back to "Adam, the son of God" (v. 38). Adam was not God's "son" in the same sense that Jesus was. Luke is telling us that Jesus is the second Adam—the new head of a new humankind.

Paul underscores just how different this new Adam is, in Philippians 2:5-11. As uncreated deity, the divine Word itself, he existed in the very form of God (v. 6). Yet he did not consider equality with God a prize to be grasped (v. 6). Instead, he emptied himself to the extreme—the Creator took on the likeness of the created being, man (v. 7).

As if that were not enough, Jesus humbled himself in obedience to God (v. 8). Not mediocre obedience or ordinary obedience—not even uncommon or unusual obedience, but obedience to the point of death (v. 8). Not a quiet and peaceful death, mind you, or even a quick and violent death. Jesus died slowly and painfully, an excruciating and humiliating death, a death alone and abandoned—death on the cross (v. 8).

Because of Jesus' faithful obedience, God raised him back to life, then raised him up to heaven, then exalted him to a position at his own right side. God gave Jesus a "name" or position higher than any in the universe besides the Father's position itself (v. 9). And God declared that some day every created being will submit to the authority of his Beloved Son who is the Last Adam, and that every created tongue will confess that Jesus is Lord (v. 10-11).

Overwhelming results. Earlier, we considered the sad effects of Adam's sin on all those whom he represented. Paul itemizes some of those effects in Romans 5. But Paul's main point in that section of Scripture is not the negative result of Adam's representation; it is the overwhelmingly positive result of Jesus' work on behalf of those whom he represents. Paul emphasizes the overwhelming nature of these good results by repeating the words "much more" again and again. Look with me at Paul's summation of Jesus' accomplishments on behalf of his people.

Paul's joy overflows as he begins: "We exult in God through our Lord Jesus Christ, "through whom we have now received the reconciliation" (Rom. 5:11). No wonder we now exult! God has reconciled us to himself! He did it outside of us, but for us—in the person of Jesus our representative. We do not have to find our lost way back to God. God has found his way to us in Jesus Christ, the Last Adam.

This reconciliation sparkles like a crown of many jewels. Paul continues:

• Although many died because of Adam's transgression, God's gift of grace increased much more to the many who are finally saved by Christ's work for them (Rom. 5:15).

• Although Adam's single sin fouled a world that was previously pure, and condemned all whom he represented, Jesus took on himself many transgressions committed by others, enabling God to "justify" or to declare right with himself all those whom Jesus represents (v. 16).

• Although death reigned over Adam's descendants through his representative transgression, all who receive the gift of righteousness through Christ reign in life much more through him as their representative (v. 17).

• Although Adam's transgression brought condemnation to all those whom he represented, Jesus' own act of righteousness culminating in his death on the cross results in justification of life to all those he represents (v. 18).

• Although Adam's personal disobedience made sinners of his descendants, Jesus' personal obedience makes his people righteous (v. 19).

So we have it: two different men, each one representing a multitude of others. Because these are representative men, each one carries on his shoulders the destiny of those whom he represents. But where the first man chooses for evil, the second man chooses for good. Two different men. Two different histories. Two different results. "As sin reigned in death [the legacy of Adam], even so grace might reign through righteousness to eternal life through Jesus Christ our Lord" (v. 21).

The final contrast. The universe will see the final contrast between these two representatives when Jesus returns and his people are either resurrected from death or transformed in life. Just as we all died once, in Adam, then all who belong to Christ will experience deathlessness in bodies that can never break down (1 Cor. 15:21-23).

We, who now have bodies like Adam's, made from earth, will then enjoy bodies like our Lord's, suited for the Age to Come (v. 42-49). So it is written, "The first man, Adam, became a living soul. The last Adam became a life-giving spirit" (v. 45). Then righteousness will fill the universe and life will replace the very memory of sin and death forever.

But Jesus is not only the new Adam. He is also new Israel—the covenant man.

Eleven

THE COVENANT MAN

Jesus not only came as the Last Adam to retrace and correct the steps of the first man. He also came as the true Israel, God's covenant People personified in a single individual life. In this one life, the New Testament tells us, we see for the first and only time a life of absolute covenant faithfulness, resulting in unbroken and unending covenant fellowship with God. Jesus hints at this in his claim to be "the true vine"—a planting which demonstrates the Father's care and produces fruit to the Father's praise (John 15:1-8). In the Old Testament, Israel had been God's "vine," but Israel had produced disappointing fruit (Isa. 5:1-7; Ps. 80:8-13).

The Psalmist prays for God to look on his people in mercy, and to raise up one who will be a faithful "vine." The Psalmist calls this individual "the man of Thy right hand," and "the son of man" (Ps. 80:14-19). Jesus fulfilled the Psalmist's prayer, and as "the son of man" he now sits at God's "right hand." The person who enjoys union with God today does so through union with Jesus, "the true vine," not by union with Israel or any other fleshly entity, including any specific Christian denomination.

Matthew also presents Jesus as the embodiment of Israel. He tells the story of Jesus in his Gospel in such a way that we see Jesus retracing the early history of Israel. We remember that Israel left Egypt as God's little "son" (Hos. 11:1), passed through the water into the wilderness to be tested for 40 years, then went to a mountain to receive God's Law.

In the same way, Matthew shows us, Jesus the Son of God left Egypt (Matt. 2:14-15), passed through the water (Matt. 3) into the wilderness to be tested for 40 days (Matt. 4), then went to a mountain to explain the true meaning of God's Law (Matt. 5-7). Jesus personifies God's covenant people. What God wanted from Israel, his stumbling covenant people, he will receive from Jesus, the faithful covenant man.

The Covenant Relationship

By the time Jesus was born, the Jewish people had enjoyed special covenant relationship with God for more than 1,200 years. Law, Land and Temple—they all symbolized and mediated a unique intimacy between this People and the Creator God. Jesus was a Jew, a descendant of Abraham and Judah and David. Merely by his physical birth from the Jewess Mary, Jesus was "born under the Law" (Gal. 4:4). From his first breath as a newborn, he shared in God's ancient covenant with Israel. Although he was the Son of God, in his humanity his relationship to God was shaped and defined by that covenant made at Sinai.

Covenant commands. The covenant relationship between God and Israel rested firmly on God's undeserved favor, as expressed by his mighty saving deeds. God had chosen Israel to be his covenant people. Faithfully remembering the promises he had made their ancestors, God had rescued Israel from slavery in Egypt.

Israel's covenant relationship required Israel to respond appropriately to God's gracious deeds. This meant keeping God's commands, living with faithful hearts in gratitude for his grace. By such faithful obedience, Israel was intended to be a light to the nations, a beacon inviting people of other nations to know the One Living God and to live in beneficial relationship with him (Ps. 67:1-7).

Covenant blessings. If Israel did keep covenant with God, they would enjoy God's covenant blessings. From Moses to Malachi, God described the benefits awaiting those who loved him and who lived with faithful hearts in fidelity to his covenant. These blessings included a stable environment, productive agriculture, peaceful society, national honor, healthy families. Most of all, the covenant-keeper would enjoy personal fellowship with God himself (Lev. 26:3-13; Deut. 28:1-14).

Covenant curses. But God's promise also carried a stern warning. If Israel disregarded the covenant, despised God's companionship and broke his commands, they would face dire and dreadful consequences (Lev. 26:15-39; Deut. 28:15-68). The covenant-breaker would encounter sudden terror and consumption. God would turn his face away. Enemies would strike down the covenant-breaker and neither heaven nor earth would deliver or respond. A sword would execute vengeance. Thirst would attack and wild animals surround. God would expel the person who broke his covenant from his presence and that cursed one would finally perish outside the land.

Jesus Fulfills the Covenant

Despite Israel's best efforts and occasional periods of revival, they never lived up to the covenant with God (Jer. 31:31-34). As the embodiment of Israel, Jesus came to fulfill all of Israel's history and Scriptures, including its divine covenant. To this end, he personally would keep the covenant commands, suffer the covenant curses and enjoy the covenant blessings.

Covenant commands. By his own faithful life, Jesus personally kept all the covenant commands. The author of Hebrews explains this in some detail, using language taken from Psalm 40. The blood of sacrificial animals can never take away sin, the Epistle writer begins (Heb. 10:4). Animal blood only symbolizes the punishment due the sinner. It can never be a substitute for what God wants most and first—a human life lived in faithful covenant obedience to God.

Unlike humans, animals are amoral creatures. Sheep and goats cannot make moral decisions. Cattle behavior is neither right nor wrong. Only a human being can give God his first choice of covenant obedience.

Jesus says as much when he comes into the world, the author of Hebrews tells us. "Sacrifice and offering You have not desired," Jesus tells the Father (quoting from Psalm 8:6-8), "but a body You have prepared for Me" (Heb. 10:5). Jesus comes to give God something better than animal sacrifices. His mission is no less than this—to give the Father a human life of faithful covenant obedience—a gift that none of God's sinful covenant people had ever managed to give.

"In whole burnt offerings and sacrifices for sin You have taken no pleasure," Jesus continues, in words from the Psalm (Heb. 10:6). Animal sacrifices were always God's second choice, never his first. God had always made that plain. "To obey is better than sacrifice," the prophet Samuel declared to disobedient Saul, after the king proposed a great sacrifice to rationalize his sin (1 Sam. 15:22). To approach God successfully, said Micah, one does not need sacrifices in huge quantities, but a humble and obedient life (Micah 6:6-8).

When God brought Israel from Egypt, he did not ask first for animal sacrifices, the prophet Jeremiah reminded Israel in his day. Instead, God asked for obedience (Jer. 7:21-23). If the people will simply obey God, Samuel and Micah and Jeremiah all are saying, they will not even need to think about offering sacrifices. Sacrifices are remedial—after disobedience. They have never been God's first choice.

Jesus came to earth as a man, to give God what he wanted most—faithful covenant obedience as a human being. "Behold, I have come," as prophesied in Scripture, he says, "to do Thy will, O God" (Heb. 10:7). The author of Hebrews now makes a subtle observation. These words from Psalm 40 first talk about animal sacrifices, he notes, then they discuss human obedience (v. 8-9). Just so, Jesus "takes away" the need for "the first" subject—animal sacrifices, "in order to establish the second"—a human life of faithful covenant obedience (v. 9).

The New Testament Scriptures repeatedly affirm Jesus' faithfulness to the Father. He is "holy, innocent, undefiled" (Heb. 7:26). He is "the Holy and Righteous One" (Acts 3:14). He is "without sin" (Heb. 4:15). He "committed no sin, neither was any deceit found in his mouth" (1 Pet. 2:22). He is God's "Lamb"—the very symbol of purity and innocence (John 1:29).

This is the achievement of Jesus. He came to do God's will in its fullness in a human life. He presented God that human life as a gift—that entire life of covenant faithfulness to God the Father—by offering his body in death on the cross. And "by this will," lived faithfully and completely throughout his human life on earth, "we have been sanctified through the offering of the body of Jesus Christ once for all" (v. 10).

Covenant curses. In his passion and his dying, Jesus personally suffered all the covenant curses. This was the scene the pious and Bible-reading Jew observed that dark day at Golgotha. Jesus has been betrayed into his enemies' hands. They have terrorized him, mocked him, flogged him, beaten him with their fists and twisted a branch of thorns and pressed it into his head (Matt. 27:26-31).

Now he hangs, nailed to a cross outside the Holy City, where he agonizes in pain and thirst until he slowly dies (John 19:28). The mocking crowd of soldiers and onlookers curse and jeer—like a band of carnivorous beasts (Matt. 27:39-44). No person on earth can help. Suddenly the sky goes dark and the earth trembles. Jesus cries out to the Father in heaven and there is no answer from above (Matt. 27:45-51).

Little wonder that Saul the learned Pharisee would conclude that Jesus was accursed (1 Tim. 1:12-13; see 1 Cor. 12:3). How could this man on the cross be a friend of God, much less the promised Messiah? This is the punishment due a transgressor—a high-handed rebel against God and his covenant. God himself must be pummeling and killing this man. It is surely clear from the Scriptures themselves!

Wrongs not his own. This is indeed the fate of a covenant-breaker, the punishment exacted on one who rebels against God. But the gospel tells us what the law could not. This punishment poured out on Jesus is for wrongs committed by others. If we will confess it, we may say with Isaiah, seven centuries before Christ:

> Surely our griefs He Himself bore,
> And our sorrows He carried;
> Yet we ourselves esteemed Him stricken,
> Smitten of God, and afflicted.
>
> But He was pierced through for our transgressions,
> He was crushed for our iniquities;
> The chastening for our well-being fell upon Him,
> And by His scourging we are healed.
>
> All of us like sheep have gone astray,
> Each of us has turned to his own way;
> But the LORD has caused the iniquity of us all
> To fall on Him. (Isa. 53:4-6)

Jesus indeed suffered the divine curses as a wrongdoer, but he "became a curse for us" (Gal. 3:13). God made Jesus, "who knew no sin, to be made sin for us" (2 Cor. 5:21). Jesus was delivered up to this death, Paul literally wrote, "because of our transgressions" (Rom. 4:25).

Covenant blessings. After Jesus had kept the covenant commands and suffered the covenant curses, he personally enjoyed all the covenant blessings. God raised him back from death, called him up into heaven and gave him a seat of honor at his own right side. There Jesus, the faithful covenant man, enjoys unhindered and unbroken fellowship in glory with God himself.

Jesus the New Covenant

Jesus did not destroy God's covenant with Israel. He personally kept all its commands. But Jesus did not obey God's covenant commands for his own benefit. He fulfilled God's requirements for all those whom he represented—for everyone who finally will be saved. Jesus did not annul the covenant commands. He embodied them into himself and preserved them, fulfilled, in his own human history.

Similarly, after Jesus had kept all the covenant commands, he stretched out his arms on the cross and suffered all the covenant curses. Again, Jesus did not endure all this for his own personal benefit. Jesus suffered as the representative of his people—all who finally will be saved. Jesus did not annul the covenant curses. They remain on display, emptied of threat or power, in the personal history of Jesus himself.

But the curses are not the final word in this story. By keeping all the covenant commands, Jesus also earned all the covenant blessings. By his faithful life, the Son of God merited the Father's highest reward—unending life in shining glory, a human being enjoying face-to-face fellowship with God. Once more, Jesus did not earn and receive all this for his own personal benefit but as representative of all his people. Just as Jesus did not annul the covenant commands and curses, neither did he annul the covenant rewards and blessings. He embodied them into his own person. He became, for all who will one day share his glory, the prototype of glorified humankind.

What does all this mean? At least this—that when God looks at Jesus, he sees his covenant perfectly fulfilled. When we look at Jesus, we see God's covenant perfectly fulfilled. We come to God, not as Adam did and as Israel did, based on our own performance or record. We come to God, now and for all eternity, based on what Jesus our representative did for us—acting in our name and on our behalf.

Let us go a step farther. By the faithful accomplishments of his doing and his dying, Jesus himself has become our new covenant (Isa. 42:6; 49:8). Each time we share the Lord's Supper, we reaffirm that relationship which he sealed with his own blood (Matt. 26:28). Jesus himself has become our righteousness (Jer. 23:6; 33:16; 1 Cor. 1:30-31).

Jesus' life, death and resurrection have become the historical and everlasting basis of our own right standing and acceptance by God. We do not ask God to look at our own record or performance. We ask God to view the record and performance of Jesus our Savior, our substitute and representative. And God promises us in the gospel that when we ask, he does exactly that.

"Can I depend on God to treat me according to what he sees in Jesus?" you might ask. "Isn't there something I must contribute?" The answers to those questions are "Yes" (to the first one) and "No" (to the second one). Both answers become obvious once we understand that when Jesus accomplished the Great Rescue, he performed a finished work.

Twelve

THE FINISHED WORK

A Triumphant Exclamation

As Jesus was dying on the cross, the Gospel of John tells us he said three final words. "It is finished." If John had written in modern English instead of first-century Greek, he likely would have ended the sentence with an exclamation mark. By these three words, Jesus announced victory, not defeat. He proclaimed a conclusion, not a concession. He declared triumph, not resignation.

God is satisfied. "It is finished!" Or better still, "It is FINISHED!" The work that sets sinners right with God here reaches its climax. The Great Rescuer has died for the sins of his people. God sees this blameless life and takes note of this sacrificial suffering. Heaven's morality and justice requires nothing else. God is perfectly satisfied, just as Isaiah the prophet had foretold some 700 years before (Isa. 53:11).

Jesus exclaims, "It is finished!" And by raising Jesus from the dead, God responds, "It is enough!" The prophet had foretold that part, too. "If He would render Himself as a guilt offering ... He will prolong His days" (Isa. 53:10). If Jesus' death was the payment for sin, his resurrection was surely God's receipt. Jesus was delivered up to death "because of our transgressions," the

New American Standard Bible literally translates, and he was raised up again "because of our justification" (Rom. 4:25).

If we ever wonder whether we are sinners, we need look only at Jesus on the cross. And if we ever wonder whether we are set right with God, we need look only at Jesus' empty tomb. Both events stand firm and unmoved—unchangeable, historical monuments to unequivocal, eternal realities.

Nothing to add. The work that put sinners right with God is complete. The old hymn tells the truth: "Jesus paid it all!" We cannot add anything to this saving work that Jesus has accomplished. We cannot improve on it. We cannot supplement it. We cannot make it shine any brighter. We cannot do anything to make God love us more than he already does. We cannot justify God's love and kindness to us any more than Jesus has justified it already.

Nothing we can ever learn, nothing we will ever do, nothing we might ever experience can contribute anything whatsoever to the work that sets us right with God. That work is the perfect doing and the perfect dying of Jesus Christ, our substitute and representative. Jesus completed that work. God accepted it and stamped it with his endorsement. The work that sets us right with God is finished. It is finished! It is FINISHED!"

A Good News Announcement

The word "gospel" means "good news." Sometimes people confuse the gospel with correct doctrine, as if it consisted of "good views." Healthy doctrine flows out of the gospel, but the gospel itself is not "good views." Others mistakenly think that the gospel is a long list of commands, as if it consisted of "good do's." The person who trusts the gospel announcement commits to follow Jesus and his teaching, but the gospel itself is not "good do's." The Law said "Do!" The gospel answers "Done!" The gospel is the "good news" that God has set sinners right with himself through Jesus Christ. It is the report of an historical event. It is the announcement of an occurrence that has already taken place.

Past tense events. New Testament writers repeatedly speak of the saving work in the past tense. God "displayed" Jesus publicly on the cross "as a propitiation" or atoning sacrifice (Rom. 3:25). God "reconciled us to Himself" through Christ (2 Cor. 5:18). "Christ redeemed us from the curse of the Law, having become a curse for us" (Gal. 3:13). In the person of Jesus Christ our representative, "we have redemption through his blood, the forgiveness of our trespasses" (Eph. 1:7). God "reconciled" us "in [Jesus'] fleshly body" (Col. 1:21-22).

God "saved us" and "abolished death" by the death and resurrection of his Son (2 Tim. 1:9-10). God's grace to sinners "has appeared" (Titus 2:11). Jesus "made purification of sins" and "obtained eternal redemption" (Heb. 1:3; 9:12). He "bore our sins" in his own body" and "by his wounds" we "are healed" (1 Pet. 2:24). The "Lion from the tribe of Judah, the Root of David, has overcome"—in the form of a slaughtered sacrificial Lamb (Rev. 5:5-6). By his sacrifice, Jesus has purchased people for God "from every tribe and tongue and people and nation" (Rev. 5:9).

Eyewitness report. The Apostle John was at the cross and at the empty tomb. "What we have heard, what we have seen with our eyes, what we beheld and our hands handled," he later wrote, "we proclaim to you also" (1 John 1:1-3). The saving accomplishments of Jesus are the good news.

Little wonder that Paul refers to this message as the good news "of your salvation" (Eph. 1:13). This gospel brings the knowledge of a hope "laid up for you in heaven" (Col. 1:5). It is the proclamation of good news. It is the certain announcement of a completed work of redemption and reconciliation and release. It is the unfolding and explanation of Jesus' last words on the cross: "It is finished!"

Jesus Has Taken His Seat

In the previous chapter we considered Jesus' life of faithful human obedience, which he then offered to God in his body on the cross. We saw how the author of the Epistle to the Hebrews analyzed that life as a representative life—a life lived in the place and stead of others. We learned that Jesus' life of human obedience counts for all his people—as the life they should have lived but did not. We also learned that Jesus, by offering his faithful, obedient life in his own human body on the cross, "sanctified" and "perfected" forever all those whom he represented and represents.

A standing job. Having said all that, the author of Hebrews now underscores the finality of Jesus' accomplishment. To do this, he compares the posture of the Jewish priests, whose offerings could not complete the task of reconciling God and sinful people, with that of Jesus—who now sits at God's right side in heaven. The unknown author first paints a picture for us of the weary Old Testament priest, forever duplicating his same, repetitive task. "Every priest stands daily ministering and offering time after time the same sacrifices, which can never take away sins" (Heb. 10:11).

The very sentence staggers with weariness. Just look at the Old Testament priest. Every day he comes to work. Every day he offers the same animal sacrifice as an offering for sin. It is a daily responsibility. He performs it again and again. It is the same sacrifice, over and over again. What is worse, there is no chance that anything will be different tomorrow. He will stand all day tomorrow. And next week. And next month—and next year. The Old Testament priest keeps standing, offering those same sacrifices, until the day he retires. Then someone else comes and stands in his place. His offering does not take away sins. These offerings will never take away sins—even after 1,000 years with hundreds of thousands of offerings presented by multiplied generations of priests.

Jesus sat down. Contrast that scene, our author continues, with what we know about Jesus. "He, having offered one sacrifice for sins for all time, sat down at the right hand of God, waiting from that time onward until His enemies be made a footstool for His feet. For by one offering He has perfected for all time those who are sanctified" (Heb. 10:12-14).

Jesus offered only one sacrifice—himself. His body represented a life of faithful human obedience to God, which is what God had always wanted but had never received. Jesus' blood was the blood of a sinless man, yet it was the penalty for sin—the sins of others. Jesus' body (obedient life) and blood (atoning sacrifice) counts for his people. God forgives their sins because of Jesus' blood. He treats them kindly because of Jesus' obedient life.

Because this sacrifice was effective, it needed to be offered only once. Because it was effective, its results endure forever. Because it was effective, Jesus could take his seat. And that is precisely what he did after God raised him from the dead and raised him up into heaven. There, God gave Jesus a seat—a seat of honor. A seat beside God himself. A right-hand seat beside the throne of the universe.

We know that the saving work is finished because Jesus, the high priest of the new covenant, has made his offering and has taken his seat in heaven. Just look what he has accomplished! Jesus' people have been "sanctified," declared holy, set apart for God, made fit to approach him whenever they please. Jesus has "perfected" them forever. They could not possibly offer God a better human life than the one Jesus has offered in their stead. They could not possibly endure a more horrible death than the one Jesus has endured on their behalf. The saving work is more than finished. It is perfect. It is everlasting.

The Great Rescue occurred in the life, death and resurrection of Jesus Christ, our substitute and God's Messiah. Because Jesus was our representative, that work happened for us—and for every person whom Jesus represented. But because the work that rescued us from sin and set us right with God happened in the person of Jesus, it also happened outside of us. For that reason, the only way we can realize the benefits of that work and enjoy them personally is by trusting in what Jesus has done.

Thirteen

Trusting is Enjoying

Only Trust Him

Because the saving work of God happened outside of us, we cannot add anything to it, improve on it, or supplement it in any way. All we can do is to trust that work. We can only rely on what Jesus did as our substitute and our representative. We can only throw ourselves on the mercy of God. This is what it means to be saved (or rescued, or delivered) "through faith."

We must tread carefully here, so that we do not distort in our own minds the role that God has assigned to faith in relation to our deliverance from sin. God does not forgive and receive us because of our faith. He does not rescue us from sin in exchange for our faith. God does not look at Jesus' faithful life and atoning death, size it all up, and then declare that one thing is still lacking in order for him to be pleased with sinners. The saving work does not consist of Jesus' obedience plus our faith.

Our faith or trust is no more a part of the grounds of God's love than our good deeds are. On the Day of Judgment, those who are saved will not swell up their chests with pride, point to their own faith and boastfully declare that they believed. No, they will kneel in humility and point to Jesus in whom they placed all their trust.

Faith is the spiritual sense of vision that looks at Jesus Christ and sees that God loves us and receives us as his own dear children. Faith is an empty hand, stretched out to receive from God what he freely gives for Jesus' sake. Faith is more accurately called an attitude than an act. It is how we always relate to God so long as we live in this space-time world. It is the principle by which we experience and enjoy any of the spiritual realities that relate to God—including the objective forgiveness and reconciliation that Jesus accomplished long ago as our representative.

As demonstrated by Jesus' representative life and death (and as justified by that same life and death), God loves sinners and treats them as his children and his friends. That is not some theoretical possibility. It is the actual reality, an accomplished fact. But, because this reality exists outside of us, we cannot experience and enjoy it except by trusting that it is true. And, because it exists for us, anyone who trusts that it is true begins to experience its reality and to enjoy its many benefits.

New Testament Declarations

Please read that last paragraph again, slowly and deliberately, noticing particularly the final two sentences. These statements are not mere theological speculations. They are not some theoretical doctrine. They describe the way things really are. We are like prisoners of war held inside a compound. But our liberator has come and has defeated our captors. Along with our freedom, he has brought truckloads of every good thing we might imagine. He has captured our enemy, taken his keys and unlocked our prison. Now he calls out to us that we are rescued. If we believe what he tells us, we can begin to live as liberated people.

The enemy in this analogy, of course, is Satan. The prison is sin. Our liberator is Jesus and the truckloads of presents are salvation in its fullness. The key to enjoying all these benefits is trust or faith. Through Jesus' victory over our enemy, everyone who believes gains access to all of God's gracious gifts (Rom. 5:2). New Testament writers affirm this truth again and again, beginning with the very words of Jesus himself.

The Gospel of John. Throughout the Gospel of John, Jesus makes a number of extraordinary promises concerning anyone who believes. He also warns of terrible consequences awaiting anyone who rejects him and refuses to believe. "Whoever puts his faith in the Son has eternal life; whoever rejects the Son will not see that life, for God's wrath remains on him" (John 3:36, NIV throughout this Gospel). Whoever believes on God through Jesus "has eternal life and will not be condemned; he has crossed over from death to life" (5:24).

It is God's will "that whoever looks to the Son and believes in him shall have eternal life, and [Jesus] will raise him up at the last day" (6:40). "If you do not believe that I am the one I claim to be," Jesus warns, "you will indeed die in your sins" (8:24). "I am the gate; whoever enters through me will be saved" (10:9). "He who believes in me will live, even though he dies; and whoever lives and believes in me will never die" (11:25-26).

The Evangelist John sums up this recurring message early in his Gospel when he writes: "For God so loved the world that he gave his one and only Son, that whoever believes in him shall not perish but have everlasting life" (3:16). John concludes on the same note, as he states his purpose for writing this Gospel. "Jesus did many other miraculous signs in the presence of his disciples which are not recorded in this book. But these are written that you may believe that Jesus is the Christ, the Son of God, and that by believing you may have life in his name" (20:30-31).

These are plain, clear statements, easy to understand. We can take them at face value. They come on the highest authority possible—from the very mouth of Jesus himself. They are recorded by one of his closest followers.

It is true that Jesus calls believers to follow him in daily life. Genuine trust does prompt obedience to the person who is trusted. Jesus' real followers will hold to his teachings, which are road markers along the highway of freedom (8:31-32). But all of that is secondary. None of it changes the more fundamental truth that we enjoy the benefits of all that Jesus has done by trusting in him. We must not ever permit any of these secondary truths to obscure, or replace, or weaken the power of the primary truth.

The primary truth is this, as viewed from two sides. First—we must trust in Jesus to experience the joy of eternal life and all the other spiritual blessings he has obtained for sinners. Second—whoever does trust in Jesus experiences all those blessings and the inexpressible joy that they bring. As surely as Jesus tells the truth, those are trustworthy statements. We can rely on them now and on the Day of Judgment.

Early Christian preaching. The early Christian preaching reaffirms Jesus' promises to anyone who believes in him. According to the Apostle Peter, in fact, such promises sum up the hope of the Old Testament prophets as well. Concerning Jesus, Peter told a house full of Romans in Caesarea, "all the prophets bear witness that through His name every one who believes in Him has received forgiveness of sins" (Acts 10:43). When a jailor in Philippi asked the Apostle Paul point blank, "What must I do to be saved?" he answered with Jesus' oft-repeated promise: "Believe in the Lord Jesus, and you shall be saved" (Acts 10:30-31).

Someone might point out that both these stories go on to include the baptism of these new believers in Jesus. That should not surprise us, as we will discuss in a later chapter, for Jesus himself commanded his Apostles to baptize those who believed on him in response to the good news of the gospel. But neither does this secondary truth change, replace or diminish the primary truths expressed by both Peter and Paul—that whoever believes on Jesus enjoys forgiveness of sins now and will be saved from God's judgment at the end of this world.

The apostolic letters. During the following years, as the Apostles wrote letters of encouragement to their young churches, they reminded their new converts of this same foundational truth. The gospel reveals God's long-awaited act of setting sinners right with himself, Paul tells the Romans. This divine accomplishment is "through faith in Jesus Christ for all those who believe" (Rom. 3:22). God's acquittal of sinners is "by faith, that it might be in accordance with grace, in order that the promise may be certain" (Rom. 4:16). In other words, we trust God's undeserved kindness and we may be sure of the results.

God once enclosed all people under sin's power, Paul tells the Galatians, so that "the promise by faith in Jesus Christ might be given to those who believe" (Gal. 3:22). We trust God from first to last, Paul explains, and "we through the Spirit, by faith, are waiting for the hope of righteousness (Gal. 5:5)."

To the Ephesians, Paul writes: "For by grace you have been saved through faith, and that not of yourselves, it is the gift of God; not as a result of works, that no one should boast" (Eph. 2:8-9).

The same Apostle opens his heart to the Philippians. His personal hope, he confesses, is "to be found in [Christ], not having a righteousness of my own derived from the Law, but that which is through faith in Christ, the righteousness which comes from God on the basis of faith" (Phil. 3:9).

Even the Old Testament Scriptures, Paul tells his protégé Timothy, give "the wisdom that leads to salvation through faith which is in Christ Jesus" (2 Tim. 3:15).

Again, it is faith from first to last, Peter reminds his scattered audience. Christ's people "are protected by the power of God through faith for a salvation ready to be revealed in the last time" (1 Pet. 1:5).

The aged Apostle John, writing to his converts, returns to the primary theme he had emphasized throughout his Gospel. "Whoever believes that Jesus is the Christ is born of God" (1 John 5:1). And, as he did in his Gospel, John tells us the purpose of his letter that we know as First John. "These things I have written to you who believe in the name of the Son of God, in order that you may know that you have eternal life" (1 John 5:13).

In a sense, therefore, John brackets the entire New Testament with this basic gospel truth. Standing near the beginning is John's Gospel, which he writes so that we may believe in Jesus and have eternal life. And standing near the ending is John's Epistle, which he writes so that we who believe may know that we have eternal life.

It is absolutely true, as we said earlier of the Gospels and the Book of Acts, that the Apostles also packed their letters with practical instructions, calls to discipleship, descriptions of the lifestyle that corresponds to faith in Jesus Christ. The apostolic letters call their readers to reflect on their own baptism and to live holy lives. They challenge new Christians to strive for spiritual maturity. They warn believers to avoid sinful practices and to perfect holiness by God's power. They encourage all of us to persevere in faith each new day, regardless of what that day may bring.

All of this is important, and all of it has its useful place. The fact remains, however, that all of this is secondary. It flows out of faith/trust in Christ. It is an evidence of salvation, not the basis for it or the ultimate means for enjoying it. As every New Testament writer would agree, the basis for God's kindness to sinners is his own unmerited love, graciously demonstrated in Jesus Christ. And the means by which sinners experience and enjoy God's love is trusting him—as also revealed in Jesus Christ.

Habakkuk said it in the Old Testament and Paul repeated it in the New: "The righteous shall live by faith" (Hab.2:4; Rom. 1:17). Our life with God is by faith from first to last. We trust him, and trust in him, every step of the way. We may be sure—as Hebrew Prophet and Christian Apostle also agree—that no one who trusts in God will ever be disappointed (Isa. 28:16; Rom. 10:11). For God has demonstrated already that he loves us—by giving his Son to die. And he has guaranteed that he forgives and receives us—by raising Jesus back from the dead.

But since we all are spiritually dead and helpless to begin with, how can anyone even trust in Christ? And if we are helpless to choose God by our own power, does that mean that God is responsible for those who are finally lost?

Fourteen

ENABLING POWER

A Striking Contrast

When we investigate the reasons why some are saved and others lost, we encounter a striking contrast. According to the Bible, those finally lost must personally accept the blame, while those who are finally saved must give God all the credit. The saved will realize some day, if they do not already know it, that even their saying "Yes" to God also resulted from his undeserved kindness and power. Jesus said it himself: "No one can come to Me, unless the Father who sent Me draws him" (John 6:44). On the other hand, "no one knows the Father" except those "to whom the Son wills to reveal him" (Matt. 11:27).

The Bible teaches that faith itself is God's gift (Eph. 2:8-9). Christians have been "graced" to believe in Christ, Paul literally wrote (Phil. 1:29). The Philippians would not be surprised to hear that, if they remembered the story of Lydia, the first convert in their own town. The Apostle Paul had come to Philippi, where he began telling the gospel story to a group of devout women who had gathered by a river to pray. Lydia, a traveling businesswoman, was in the group. As she listened to Paul, "the Lord opened her heart to respond" (Acts 16:14).

God fully accomplished the Great Rescue of sinners in the doing and dying of Jesus. From that time forward, he also applies that rescue to those who hear the gospel and who do not say "No" to the good news of God's grace. By God's kindness and power, he enables all those people—one by one—to truly and freely say "Yes!"

Conversion involves the human intellect, but it does not rest on human wisdom or logic. It involves the human will, to be sure, but it does not originate in that fallen will. It involves a human decision—a genuine, authentic decision that occurs in earth-time history—but that decision does not depend on human power. Whenever we see someone come to faith in Christ, we may know that God is at work. The conversion of a fallen sinner is a divine work.

The Bible describes this divine work of conversion by a variety of metaphors. Believers, the Bible tells us, are people who enjoy a new heart, a new birth, a new life, and a new creation.

A New Heart

Some 600 years before Jesus, God spoke to the prophet Ezekiel, then in exile in Babylon, about a time of blessing in the distant future. God has punished his people, he reminds the prophet, by sending them into exile in Assyria (from the northern kingdom of Israel) and in Babylon (from the southern kingdom of Judah). They have been "scattered among the nations" (Ezek. 36:19). But God has not forgotten his people. He will bring them back from among the nations to their own land— to show that he is God (v. 22-24).

Different interpretations. Christian scholars interpret promises like this one in different ways. One group notes the literal fulfillment of other prophecies and insists that God will literally fulfill this promise as well, by restoring scattered Jews once again to the ancient Promised Land. Some conclude that this happened in the returns led by Zerubbabel, Ezra and

Nehemiah. Others see it occurring in present-day Israel. Others anticipate it as still an entirely-future event.

Another group of scholars notes that New Testament writers sometimes quote such literal-sounding prophecies, then point to their fulfillment in the saving work of Jesus Christ and the conversion of Jews and even Gentiles to him. These scholars also believe that God's promises are true, but that their meaning is often understood only in retrospect after God has fulfilled them, sometimes in ways that we least expect.

A greater work. Whatever the case concerning the land, God's greater work is not limited to external geography; it involves the hearts, minds and consciences of the people themselves. "I will sprinkle clean water on you … I will cleanse you from all your filthiness" (v. 25). Whether Ezekiel foresaw Gentiles in this prophecy or not, its language states the truth concerning Jews and Gentiles alike, for the way of salvation is the same for all. But this picture is still not complete, for God promises to do more than forgive.

"I will give you a new heart," he promises, "and put a new spirit within you." This is nothing less than a spiritual heart transplant. "I will remove the heart of stone and give you a heart of flesh" (v.26). In place of a spiritual nature as dead as rocks, God will give his people spiritual life that responds to him and interacts with him as Creator and Savior. "I will put my Spirit within you and cause you to walk in My statutes, and you will be careful to observe My ordinances" (v. 27). This is nothing less than the new covenant predicted by Jeremiah and fulfilled by Jesus Christ (Jer. 31:31-34; Heb. 8:6-13).

A radical accomplishment. Seen in this light, conversion to Christ is a radical accomplishment indeed. It is more than a human decision to try to live for Christ. It is more than temporary forgiveness. It is far more than joining a church, or going through some ritual, or making new resolutions. Conversion means receiving a new heart—removing a stone-hard mind toward God and replacing it with a tender, living spiritual heart. It means that we do not depend any longer on our own intentions and efforts to please God, for God has given us a new source of power in his Spirit who resides in us.

This also means that conversion is not an end in itself— some kind of trophy moment in our relationship with God that we place on a display shelf and only remember thereafter. Conversion is instead the beginning of a new life—a life of obedience, of praise and worship, of good deeds, of growing to resemble the character of Jesus Christ—as many New Testament passages describe our new life in the Spirit.

A New Birth

Closely related to the word picture of a new heart is the metaphor of a new birth. This metaphor arose during a well-known conversation between Jesus and a certain Jewish leader named Nicodemus. The name "Nicodemus" means "victor over the people" and, by all accounts, Nicodemus had managed to conquer his obstacles and rise to a position of honor and success. But when he talked to Jesus, Nicodemus learned the limits of his own heritage and human ability. The story unfolds in John's Gospel, chapter three.

A Pharisee's preconceptions. Nicodemus was a prominent man, both religiously and socially (John 3:1). Religiously, he belonged to the Pharisees, whose strict orthodoxy and public piety was obvious to all. He was also a "ruler" of the Jews, a member of the Jewish Sanhedrin or high court. And he was himself a spiritual teacher—the Greek says "the teacher"—of Israel (v. 10). Although Nicodemus later became more openly devoted to Jesus, their first encounter happened at night—both in terms of the clock and in terms of Nicodemus' depth of spiritual understanding (v. 2).

Nicodemus addresses Jesus respectfully as "Rabbi" and acknowledges from Jesus' miraculous signs that he has come from God (v. 2). But Jesus sees Nicodemus' heart and knows that this Pharisee's shallow faith, though awed by signs, is not nearly deep enough (1:23-25). Jesus also knows that Nicodemus assumes that he merits a reserved place in God's kingdom since he is a pious, leading descendant of Abraham.

A drastic need. Based on what he sees in Nicodemus' heart, Jesus turns all of this Pharisees' preconceptions upside-down with one stark pronouncement: "Truly, truly, I say to you, unless one is born again, he cannot see the kingdom of God" (v. 3). It is not enough to be an Israelite. It is not sufficient to be a Pharisee. Entrance into God's kingdom—which means life with God now and in the Age to Come—requires more even than being a teacher and ruler in Israel.

What is required is a new birth, regeneration by God himself. The word translated "again" in this verse literally means "from above." Since every living person already has been born into this world, to be born from above is also to be born "again." Nicodemus misunderstands Jesus' meaning and asks how a man can re-enter his mother's womb for a second birth (v. 4). Jesus re-emphasizes his original point that a different kind of birth is required. "Unless one is born of water and the Spirit, he cannot enter into the kingdom of God" (v. 5).

Then Jesus explains what he means. "That which is born of the flesh is flesh; and that which is born of the Spirit is spirit" (v. 6). The first birth originates with human flesh and involves a fleshly entrance into this world. It is a birth of (from, out of) "water"—the sac of amniotic fluid that served as our home during the time we were being formed. And although that process is so awesome that it borders on the miraculous, what is born from and generated by flesh still will be flesh. A spiritual nature suited for God's kingdom requires a spiritual origin—regeneration by the Spirit of God himself. That "birth" of the Spirit must come from above.

This truth applies not only to Nicodemus, for "you" here is literally plural in form. You—all of you—teachers, rulers, Pharisees,

Israelites in general, Gentiles as well—must be born again from above. We all must experience spiritual rebirth if we are to enjoy God's kingdom that transcends what is earthly and fleshly.

A heavenly mystery. Although the need for spiritual rebirth is obvious, regeneration by God's Spirit involves mystery beyond our comprehension. You cannot even explain the wind, Jesus tells Nicodemus, but can only see its effects (v. 8). Jesus makes a holy pun here, for "wind" and "Spirit" both translate the same word in Greek.

Spiritual regeneration is not something we do for ourselves or bring about by our own power and effort (v. 14-16). Jesus' statement "You must be born again" is not a command for us to obey. It is a spiritual reality for us to acknowledge. The new birth from above does not originate in any human source, impulse or decision, but in the exercise of the will of God (John 1:13; James 1:18). Yet it is the personal, actual experience of anyone who believes in Jesus—for whoever believes in him has eternal life (John 3:14-16).

A New Life

The Apostle Paul describes the miracle of conversion in still another way—as a resurrection from the dead. This story involves three realities, as Paul tells it in Ephesians 2:1-10. He expresses these realities by three participial phrases that portray three separate scenes: (1) "You, being dead"... (2) God, being rich in mercy"... and (3) You, being saved ones by grace through faith" (v. 1, 4, 8).

Dead in sin. In our natural sinful condition, we belong in the spiritual cemetery (v. 1-3). As fallen people, sinners with our ancestor Adam, we are as dead as corpses. We follow Satan, live according to the course of the present evil age, act out of our fleshly desires and naturally do things that bring God's wrath in response. The first scene is grim: "You, being dead in your trespasses and sins" (v. 1).

God rich in mercy. But God has not abandoned us to our natural state and end. He is rich in mercy and full of love (v. 4). When we were dead and hopeless, he stepped in to rescue us from our present condition and ultimate destiny. He did this through the death and resurrection of Jesus, our representative and Savior. God gave us to his Son before the world began and what happened to him happened also to us.

When Jesus rose from the dead, so did we (v. 5). When Jesus ascended to heaven, so did those whom he represented. When Jesus took his seat of honor at God's side in heaven, so did all who would finally be saved (v. 6). Only in the coming Age will we fully realize the grace and kindness of God to sinners in his Son (v. 7). The second scene is thrilling and joyful: "God, being rich in mercy" (v. 4).

Saved by grace. By the work of Christ, God has radically transformed our situation for good. No longer are we dead in trespasses and sins. Now we are "saved ones, by grace through faith," as verse eight actually states. This one verse summarizes in a few, single-syllable words the story of the Bible and the truth of the gospel. We have been rescued. It happened outside of us, in the representative doing and dying of Jesus Christ.

God accomplished that for his own glory and according to his own plan and purpose. We did not make it happen. We do not deserve it. The saving work does not rest on our own knowledge or will. It does not depend on our own power or effort. It is God's free gift. We need only to trust it to enjoy it. It is ours for the believing. The third scene is delightful: "You, being saved ones, by grace through faith" (v. 8).

To be converted to Christ is to be raised from death to life. Only God can raise the dead. And he does!

A New Creation

We may also think of conversion as a repetition of the Bible's opening story. There we saw God create from nothing everything that now exists. Even so, Paul literally writes, "If anyone is in Christ, there is a new creation; the old things passed away; behold, new things have come." This, too, is the work of the Creator God (2 Cor. 5:17-18).

After God spoke the universe into existence, he commanded and there was light. In the same way, "God, who said, 'Light shall shine out of darkness,' is the One who has shone in our hearts to give the light of the knowledge of the glory of God in the face of Christ" (2 Cor. 4:6). God has expelled the darkness of sin. The Light of the World now illuminates our minds, warms our hearts and brightens our lives. One day the Sun of Righteousness will return to destroy evil completely and to make his people dance with joy forever (Mal. 4:1-3).

When God had completed his creation, he surveyed all that he had made and found it very good. Then, that work completed, God rested. In the same way, "we who have believed, enter that rest," for Jesus has accomplished the saving work—and it is very good (Heb. 4:3). The saving deeds of Jesus are too good, in fact, to keep quiet about. Anything this wonderful deserves to be celebrated in public and shared with others. And that is exactly what happens in gospel baptism, when faith goes formal.

Fifteen

FAITH GOES FORMAL

An Assumed Experience

By being baptized in water, a new believer points to the finished work of Christ and publicly declares that he or she trusts in that work alone for right standing with God. Baptism is about Jesus from first to last. And despite all the controversies that have swirled around this topic through the centuries, when we read the New Testament itself we discover that disputes about baptism are noticeably absent. Unfortunately, the same cannot be said about later church history, including the Christian world today.

Two modern extremes. When it comes to baptism's meaning and purpose, Christian people hold a wide variety of views. At one extreme is the view that baptism itself causes God's forgiveness, spiritual cleansing, membership in Christ's body and other gifts of grace. According to this view, whenever a proper person performs the proper action and says the proper words in baptism, God always pours out his grace on the baptized person.

Those holding this view sometimes say that no one can possibly enjoy God's grace apart from baptism, and that baptism conveys grace whether faith is present or not. They see baptism, not faith, as the means for enjoying grace. They do not ask someone if he or she trusts in Jesus as Savior, but whether or not that person has been baptized.

At the other extreme, and usually in reaction against the view above, is the view that baptism has absolutely nothing to do with receiving God's grace. According to this view, baptism is a rather minor command of Christ, useful only as a rite of initiation into a local congregation. It certainly has no relationship to the gospel, no reference to Christ, no connection to faith, and nothing to do with any spiritual blessing. The person holding this view hesitates to tell others that they need to be baptized, and, truth be told, is mildly embarrassed by many passages of Scripture that address the subject.

Neither of these views accurately reflects the New Testament's teaching about baptism. Both of them, in fact, share the same error—they do not view baptism in the light of Jesus himself. For those who wrote the New Testament, everything important finds its importance in relation to Jesus Christ.

Shared in common. It is fair to say that New Testament writers take baptism for granted. They assume that Christian converts are baptized. They command baptism of those who have not received it, report baptisms as they occur, and explain the implications of baptism after the fact. But they never argue about baptism with each other.

Indeed, this passive event—the person obeying this command *receives* baptism—is one of those shared realities that the Apostle Paul considers common to the Christian experience. "There is one body and one Spirit," he writes to the Ephesians, "just as also you were called in one hope of your calling; one Lord, one faith, one baptism, one God and Father of all who is over all and through all and in all" (Eph. 4:4-6).

Ordained by Jesus Himself

We need not be surprised that Christians in the New Testament share the experience of baptism in common, for Jesus personally ordained that those who believe the gospel should be baptized. Shortly before he ascended to heaven, Jesus charged his trained band of followers to make disciples throughout the world from that time forward.

According to Matthew. "All authority has been given to Me in heaven and on earth," announced the Son of Man, soon to sit at God's right side. "Go therefore and make disciples of all the nations, baptizing them in the name of the Father and the Son and the Holy Spirit, teaching them to observe all that I commanded you; and lo, I am with you always, even to the end of the age" (Matt. 28:18-20). This commission is remarkably clear and quite encompassing. The one who has *all* authority calls for the discipling of *all* the nations, teaching them *all* of his instructions and promising his own presence throughout *all* time.

According to Mark. This becomes even clearer in Mark's account of Jesus' evangelistic assignment, as preserved in several ancient texts and found in some English translations. Although the earliest Greek manuscripts close Mark's final chapter with verse eight, some manuscripts include several additional verses beyond verse eight. Nestled among those later verses, roughly parallel to the commission in Matthew, Jesus tells the Apostles: "Go into all the world and preach the gospel to all creation. He who has believed and has been baptized shall be saved; but he who has disbelieved shall be condemned" (Mark 16:15-16).

Like its parallel text in Matthew's Gospel, this passage calls for worldwide evangelization. Where Matthew has "make disciples," Mark says to "preach the gospel." And where Matthew includes baptism as a command for the evangelist to fulfill, Mark states a promise of Jesus to the one who believes and is baptized. Jesus mentions two possible responses to the gospel:

to disbelieve and reject it; or to believe and be baptized. In this contrast, the focus is on believing. Jesus assumes that those who believe will be baptized.

Three observations. Based on these two Gospels, we may confidently say three things. First, baptism rests on the authority of Jesus, to whom God has given all authority in heaven and on earth. Second, it is an ordained response to the preaching of the gospel. Third, it is assumed of those who believe the gospel and who wish to become followers of Jesus the Christ.

Since baptism rests on Jesus' authority, we dare not minimize it or treat it as something merely optional. Since Jesus ordained it as a response to gospel preaching, those who proclaim the gospel need always to make their hearers aware of that fact. Since the Gospels assume that believers who follow Jesus will be baptized, we should never leave anyone with the impression that believers can follow Jesus faithfully while ignoring this gospel ordinance.

The person who is baptized follows Jesus by obeying his command. That individual also follows Jesus in a literal sense as Jesus himself was baptized. The meaning of our baptism is related in a special way to the meaning of his.

Jesus' Baptism—His Public Identification

John the Baptist. The Gospels describe the work of John the Baptist, whom God sent to prepare the way for Jesus by calling Israel to repentance (Mark 1:1-3). John preached in the Judean Wilderness. He probably was acquainted with the Qumran community, a centuries-old Jewish sect which wrote the Dead Sea Scrolls and itself practiced ritual washings. John stood, as it were, with one foot on Old Testament soil and the other foot on New Testament soil.

Throughout Israel's history, the prophets called the erring people to repent—to turn their straying minds back toward God. John the Baptist demanded the same response from the

Jews of his day. As a demonstration of that change of heart, John preached "a baptism of repentance for the forgiveness of sins" (Mark 1:4). Those who repented at John's preaching expressed their repentance by being baptized in the Jordan River, "confessing their sins" (v. 5).

Jesus in the sinner line. Just as ancient Jewish worshipers confessed their sins while laying their hands on the heads of sacrificial animals to ceremonially transfer their sins to the animal, so we might picture John's converts standing in the Jordan River, confessing their sins, ceremonially leaving them in the water when they themselves climbed out. The confessions covered the spectrum of sinners—tax-gatherers, soldiers and common people alike (Lk. 3:10-18).

We can only imagine John's surprise that day when Jesus, the sinless Son of God, walked into this line of sinners (Lk. 3:21-22). John knew who Jesus was, and he knew that Jesus did not belong in the sinner line. "You should be baptizing me," the prophet protested in effect. But Jesus insisted. "It is fitting for us" to do this, he said, "to fulfill all righteousness" (Matt. 3:13-15).

So John baptized Jesus in the River Jordan, and all heaven broke loose in celebration. The heavens opened, the Spirit of God descended and rested on Jesus like a dove, and God declared in an audible voice that Jesus was his Son who pleased him very much (Mark 1:9-11).

John knew his Scriptures and he made the connections between these events and Old Testament prophecies. Jesus is the Son of God, the Servant Messiah, the Suffering Servant of Isaiah 53. Based on the events at Jesus' baptism, John began to introduce Jesus to the people: "Behold, the Lamb of God who takes away the sin of the world!" (John 1:26-36.) This, John later said, was why God sent him to baptize—in order that Jesus "might be manifested" as the divine Savior who would become the sacrifice for sin (John 1:31).

Using sanctified imagination, we may picture the sinless Jesus going down into the sin-filled Jordan, then coming out with all these sins of others clinging to his own body. As the sacrifice appointed by the Father, Jesus carried our sins in his own body to the cross (1 Pet. 2:24; see Isa. 53:6, 11-12).

The journey to the cross began that day at the Jordan, when Jesus was baptized and was publicly identified as the Lamb of God. This baptism in water marked the beginning of Jesus' saving work. That work would climax with his baptism in blood (Lk. 12:50).

Jesus' baptism and ours. Jesus' baptism identified him publicly as the divine Savior, the Lamb of God who takes away the sin of the world. Our baptism identifies us publicly as people who trust in Jesus as our atoning sacrifice and personal Savior. We see this relationship in Luke's story of the Ethiopian treasury official, whom Philip encountered on the Jerusalem-Gaza highway (Acts 8:26-36). Philip found the Ethiopian reading Isaiah's prophecy of one who would die as a sacrificial Lamb, and he explained that the prophet was speaking about Jesus. The Ethiopian trusted in Jesus and immediately asked to be baptized. His inward faith prompted its outward expression.

In gospel baptism, our faith dresses up in formal attire and attends a spiritual ball. By this ceremony, we publicly trust Christ and him alone for all the benefits of his perfect doing and dying (Mark 16:16; Col. 2:12). In baptism we openly formalize the faith in our hearts—the faith that receives with empty hands the full outpouring of God's wondrous gift of grace.

Because baptism expresses faith—and because faith receives God's grace—the New Testament writers do not hesitate to mention in connection with baptism an entire colorful rainbow of spiritual blessings. Baptism, it is fair to say, *signifies* all these spiritual blessings that are ours by faith in Jesus Christ. It is a *sign* that points to Christ and to all his blessings. It is therefore a very *significant* event (in the most literal sense of that word) in the life of any believer.

Blessings Signified by Baptism

Forgiveness. The first sermon Luke reports in his story of the earliest church was to Jewish pilgrims from throughout the Roman world who had come to Jerusalem to celebrate the harvest festival of Pentecost (Acts 2). God sends the Holy Spirit upon Jesus' waiting disciples and they hear a sound like a mighty wind. Tongues of fire appear in the air and rest on each of them. A crowd of curious onlookers gathers, only to hear Jesus' followers speaking in a variety of languages they had never studied or learned.

Peter tells the story of Jesus, and his conscience-stricken audience interrupts and asks what to do (v. 37). Peter tells them all to repent and commands every one of them to be baptized "in the name of Jesus Christ"—that is, in recognition of his position as Lord and Christ at God's right side in heaven (v. 38). This response is "for the forgiveness of sins," a blessing also tied to repentance in Luke's account of Jesus' final commission (Lk. 24:46-47).

Neither Peter nor Luke was embarrassed to link repentance and baptism to forgiveness of sins, for both clearly understood that God forgives people based on the atonement that Jesus has made, and that sinners can only trust him for that forgiveness. Through Jesus' name, Peter later tells the Roman officer Cornelius and his house full of relatives and friends, "every one who believes in Him has received forgiveness of sins" (Acts 10:43).

As faith embodied in ritual, baptism stands as a signpost pointing to Jesus and announcing that sins are forgiven. It "signifies" this blessing—openly declares it—officially announces it. In doing so, baptism does not point to itself or to our faith. It points to Jesus in whom our faith is placed.

Receiving the Holy Spirit. At Pentecost, Peter promised that
God will give the Holy Spirit to anyone who repents and is baptized in Jesus' name, a phrase which here literally means out of
respect for him (Acts 2:38). This gift is God's own personal powerful Presence (Acts 5:32). Elsewhere we read that the Holy
Spirit is received by hearing the gospel with faith (Gal. 3:5). Yet
Peter and Paul do not contradict each other on this point, for
baptism embodies faith. Because baptism is faith formalized,
baptism also signifies this blessing which faith receives.

Although baptism signifies receiving God's Spirit, God is
free to work on any timetable he pleases. Within this same
book of Acts, the Holy Spirit sometimes comes before water
baptism (10:44-46) and sometimes after it (8:14-17). Whatever
the order of events in specific cases, the various scenarios regularly include the same elements of the gospel preached, faith
in response, baptism as faith's expression and the gift of the
Holy Spirit.

Salvation. Jesus himself promised that the one who
believes and is baptized will be saved (Mark 16:16). So that we
do not attribute salvation to baptism itself (or even to faith),
Jesus follows his promise with a contrasting warning: the one
who understands the gospel and refuses to believe it will be
condemned. As we have noted already, the choice is to believe
or to disbelieve. Baptism then formally expresses the faith of
the person who believes.

We see this in the story of the jailor at Philippi, to whom
Paul promised: "Believe in the Lord Jesus, and you shall be
saved, you and your household" (Acts 16:31). As the story continues, Paul relates the message of the Lord in more detail, and
the jailor and his household are all baptized (v. 32-33). That
done, they "rejoiced greatly, having believed in God" (v. 34).

Similarly, Scripture says that whoever calls upon the name
of the Lord will be saved (Rom. 10:13). In context, this statement summarizes the earlier promise that "if you confess with

your mouth Jesus as Lord, and believe in your heart that God raised Him from the dead, you shall be saved" (v. 9). This passage, as nearly as any other, provides a biblical basis for asking converts to pray "the sinner's prayer"—something (perhaps surprisingly to many) not directly mentioned in any New Testament conversion story. What we do find, in the account of Paul's own conversion to Christ, is Ananias' instruction to Saul of Tarsus to "Arise, and be baptized; and wash away your sins, calling on His name" (Acts 22:16).

In baptism one formally calls on Jesus to save, embodying in this ceremonial event the prayer of one's heart and lips. This public event does not detract from salvation through faith. Instead, by pointing to Jesus, it emphasizes and underscores that faith is looking to Jesus and is trusting in him alone to save. Hoping in Christ, the baptized believer enjoys a clean conscience (Heb. 10:22-23).

Union with Christ. When Paul wants to urge new Christians to live a godly life, he reminds them of their baptism (Rom. 6:1-10). They were "baptized into Christ" and "into His death" (v. 3). The larger truth is that Jesus' people were joined to him already in God's eyes when Jesus personally died, was buried and rose again, for "we died with Christ," our representative, and "our old self was crucified with Him" (v. 6, 8). What happened to Jesus also happened to his people, because he represented them (Col. 2:13-15).

Baptism signifies this union with Christ—it is a "likeness" of his death and resurrection (v. 7). In this visible ritual of baptism, those who are children of God by faith in Christ Jesus are formally and officially "clothed with Christ" himself (Gal. 3:26-27; see also Col. 2:14). Because we are joined to Christ—a reality which baptism formalizes and signifies—it is only appropriate that we should live "in newness of life" (Rom. 6:4; Col. 3:1-5).

Separation from the world. On Pentecost, Peter exhorted his audience to separate, or "save" themselves, from their unbelieving generation (Acts 2:40). About 3,000 people did this by receiving Peter's words and being baptized (v. 41). Peter later makes the same point by comparing baptism to the Flood waters that decisively separated Noah from his wicked contemporaries (1 Pet. 3:20-22).

Noah was a righteous man who walked with God by faith in a very wicked world (Gen. 6:5, 9; Heb. 11:7). But Noah's faith, and God's approval of Noah because of it, were not immediately obvious to every casual bystander. God knew that faithful Noah was different from his unbelieving neighbors, for he saw their hearts. The water of the Flood made a clear separation between Noah and the unbelievers around him. The water made obvious to all what God already knew—that Noah did not belong with that wicked crowd. By making that distinction, the Flood water "saved" or rescued Noah from an unbelieving world.

In the same sense, Peter says, "baptism now saves you." Not from sin, according to this verse, but—as in Noah's case—from the wicked world. In baptism, the new believer formally appeals to God for a good conscience, based on Jesus' victorious resurrection, ascension and exaltation at God's right side in heaven (1 Pet. 3:21-22). Baptism signifies a separation from the unbelieving world, based on the finished work of Jesus in which we place our hope.

Union with Christ's people. Baptism also identifies the believer as belonging to the Christian community, the universal church of Jesus Christ. To belong to Christ is to become Abraham's spiritual offspring—a family of faith that includes people from all nations, social categories and genders (Gal.3:28-29).

When believers at Corinth selected their favorite teachers and formed mini-denominations based on those choices, the Apostle Paul reprimanded them with a series of rhetorical questions. "Has Christ been divided? Paul was not crucified for you, was he? Or were you baptized in the name of Paul?" (1 Cor. 1:13.)

Baptism is a sign of unity within the whole body of Christ. It is not a marker for membership in some sect. It is Christ's ordinance, not the ordinance of any denomination. To be baptized is not to join a segment of Christ's body or to become affiliated with any partisan wing of the universal church. Baptism signifies that the person being baptized takes his or her place as a member of Christ's body. To be baptized is to be publicly identified as a part of the one holy, apostolic, universal or "catholic" (in the original sense) church of Jesus Christ.

Today it is quite common for people to question the need for church. That is not surprising, if these questioners think of "church" as a stodgy old religious institution obsessed with rules and raising money but largely irrelevant to the concerns of everyday life.

But how would these same people respond to a community of Jesus' followers who, like their Leader, lived to glorify God and to help others come to know him; who valued individuals more highly than money; who measured greatness in terms of service to others? Would they be surprised to learn that Jesus intended the Great Rescue to result in just that kind of "church"—a community in which he himself would also live by his Spirit?

Sixteen

SPIRIT-FILLED COMMUNITY

Jesus' Own Vision

An advance peek. Jesus himself envisioned his followers as a community of faith—a fellowship that would provide the world a sneak preview of God's coming reign in the kingdom of heaven. God, not man, will usher in this reign in its fullness, and Jesus taught his disciples to pray for it in three parallel expressions. "Our Father in heaven," we ask: "Your name, may it be hallowed; your kingdom, may it come; your will, may it be done—[all three] as in heaven, so on earth" (Matt. 6:9-10, Greek).

This all will happen universally in the world to come, in the new heavens and new earth. Then every living being in the universe will fully recognize God's holiness and do exactly what he wishes, making his reign a total reality. Jesus' plan is for those things to begin now, within the community of those who trust and follow him. His disciples therefore pray: "Yours *is* the kingdom, and the power, and the glory" (Matt. 6:13). This phrase also means that in the community of Jesus' followers, God sets the agenda, supplies the energy and means to carry it out, and receives all the credit for the results.

The ekklesia. Jesus sometimes spoke of this community as his *ekklesia*, a Greek word usually translated in the New

Testament as "church." Jesus did not invent this word. Greek-speaking people in the first-century regularly used the term—which literally means an "assembly"—for their town-meetings. Luke also uses *ekklesia* when telling of one such meeting in the city of Ephesus (Acts 19:32, 39, 41).

Far more important, hundreds of years before Jesus, the translators of the Greek Old Testament had chosen the word *ekklesia* to represent the Hebrew word for the "assembly" or "congregation" of the ancient People of God. Luke uses *ekklesia* once in that sense as well (Acts 7:38).

By choosing the word *ekklesia*, Jesus reminds us that the Israelites did not slip out of Egypt one by one, to wander in isolation in the wilderness until they individually entered the Promised Land. God delivered an enormous crowd from Egyptian bondage and baptized them in the Red Sea and a column of cloud, making them one People under Moses. Similarly, Jesus, having rescued his People from sin and death, baptizes them in the Holy Spirit and makes them one community in him (1 Cor. 10:1-4; 12:13). As leaders of his new community, Jesus commissioned twelve Apostles, an intentional number which reminds us also of the twelve tribes of Israel.

Jesus speaks of this community most clearly in Matthew 16:18, in response to Peter's confession of the divinely-revealed truth that Jesus is the Messiah-Christ and God's Son. "Upon this rock" foundation, Jesus says, speaking of the truth Peter had just expressed, "I will build my *ekklesia*."

The little word "my" is very important here. Like Israel before, this new community (made up of Jews and non-Jews alike) will be God's People. Unlike Israel, this community will consciously relate to God through the person and work of Jesus himself. And because Jesus will rise from the grave victorious over Death, Jesus promises that even Death can never overcome his People. "The gates of Hades shall not overpower her," he literally says.

Life in community. Many scholars believe that the Gospel of Matthew was written originally for an early Christian community, who used it as a manual for living together as the People of Jesus. Whether that is the case or not, this Gospel includes much instruction from Jesus about life together in community. As Jesus envisions it, this will be a learning community, taught by instructors who follow Jesus themselves (Matt. 5:19; 7:15-21). Like Jesus the Master, his community will be marked by humble service. The greatest in this community will be those who greatly serve (20:25-28; 23:11-12).

Members of this community will love each other, as one of their highest priorities (22:39). When a community-member falls into sin, fellow-members will be slow to condemn but quick to forgive (7:1-5; 18:15-22). This community will not be closed and exclusive, but ever-expanding—making disciples of all the nations (28:18).

Jesus does not expect his disciples to create such a community by their own wisdom or power. Matthew's Gospel closes with the promise: "I am with you always, even to the end of the age" (Matt. 28:20). Just as the Father directed and empowered Jesus' own ministry by the Holy Spirit, so Jesus, through the same Holy Spirit, will guide and enable his community until the end of time. Wherever even two or three gather in his name, Jesus promises to be present (Matt. 18:20).

Each local church today can measure its own faithfulness and progress by Jesus' description of his intended community. If a congregation does not resemble that description, regardless of how exciting or successful or prosperous or growing it might be, it has missed the divine agenda and has lost touch with our Lord. Jesus once addressed a church that considered itself rich and self-sufficient, but he saw it as "wretched and miserable and poor and blind and naked" (Rev. 3:17).

The Earliest Community

Christ's community has never fully measured up to his intentions for it, not even the earliest Christian community as revealed in the Book of Acts. Luke does not idealize that story or paint the picture in rosy colors. Jesus' first disciples, like his followers today, were real people. At times, they resembled the community in Jesus' vision. At other times they did not.

Real people. On the positive side, we see people learning together, praying together, eating together, sharing together (Acts 2:42). The group increases, as God adds new converts to their number (2:47). They adapt to new situations, providing fresh structures and methods to meet new needs (6:1-6). When doctrinal issues threaten to divide their unity, they seek solutions in prayerful conference—listening to Scripture, looking to Jesus, observing what God is doing in their own time and experience (chap. 15). Eventually they carry the gospel throughout the Roman world. Jesus' words are fulfilled: "Upon this rock I will build my church."

These real people also included notable sinners. Luke's story involves racists and grumblers, self-seekers and liars, sectarians and legalists. God sometimes works through such individuals. He always accomplishes his work despite them and their sinful ways.

The Holy Spirit at work. Most of all, the Book of Acts is a story of the Holy Spirit at work—empowering, guiding, directing, preserving. Luke begins this book by referring to his Gospel "about all that Jesus began to do and teach" (Acts 1:1). We may fairly say that Acts, Luke's second volume, is about all that Jesus continued to do and teach—present among his followers through the Holy Spirit. Some have even referred to this book as "The Acts of the Holy Spirit." You only have to read through Acts to understand why.

The Spirit arranges appointments between individuals who are eager to hear God's gospel and others who can tell it. God opens hearts to understand, opens timid mouths to speak and opens doors of opportunity for the two to coincide. More than once, he opens prison doors to release his own people and to thwart his enemies. Sometimes God allows his own people to be killed—but Jesus in heaven stands in honor of one of them named Stephen, the first to die for his sake. Jesus' words are fulfilled: "The gates of Hades shall not prevail against her."

The great evangelistic trips reported throughout the second half of Acts do not begin in great human planning but in fervent prayer and in the impetus of God's Spirit. These missions are carried out, not by extraordinary human skills of organizing, fund-raising or follow-up, but by constant sensitivity to God's leading and ongoing obedience to his Spirit.

Indeed, if we remove the supernatural from the Book of Acts, very little remains. What God assigns, he also empowers and accomplishes. The disciples' prayer is true: "Yours is the kingdom, and the power, and the glory." It is still true today, throughout the world—wherever Christian communities seek God's agenda, cooperate with it in God's strength, and give God all the credit. It does not matter whether those communities are two or three disciples in size, or three hundred or three thousand. God's work does not ultimately depend on human resources in any quantity, but on his own purpose and power and grace.

Portraits of Community

New Testament writers use a variety of word-pictures to describe the community of Christ's followers. Like *ekklesia*, they borrow many of these figures from the Old Testament. Each of these terms portrays some special aspect or trait of the Christian community. All of them draw meaning from Jesus and the Great Rescue he has accomplished for his People.

Temple. Just as Jesus used the language of building and architecture when he promised Peter, "Upon this rock I will build my church," so Peter describes God's community as a temple under construction, composed of living stones (1 Pet. 2:4-8). Although Peter's name means "rock," Jesus himself is the cornerstone of this spiritual building, as foretold by Old Testament prophets (Isa. 8:14; 28:16; Psalm 118:22).

Peter knew these ancient prophecies, and he referred to them in his preaching and in his writing (Acts 4:11-12). Human beings may build grand cathedrals to the glory of God, but the Creator's temple today does not consist of physical stones. Jesus is building his temple of "living stones," one person at a time, as individuals believe the gospel and begin to follow him.

Peter calls believers to the same kind of community life Jesus had envisioned. He portrays a community that prays fervently to God (1 Pet. 4:7), whose members love each other and show that love by hospitality and mutual service (4:8-11). They live in imitation of Christ, even when persecuted (2:21-23; 4:12-14). As God provides opportunity, believers share the gospel with all who indicate a willingness to hear (3:15-16).

Paul also describes the Christian community as God's temple. Just as God filled the desert Tabernacle and Solomon's Temple with his Presence, symbolized by the cloud of divine glory, so God now fills the believing community with his Presence in the Holy Spirit (1 Cor. 3:16). The Spirit lives in each individual believer as well, but Paul here refers to the People of God in community when he asks: "Do you not know that you [plural] are a temple of God, and that the Spirit of God dwells in you?" Jesus continues to build this temple, Paul tells the Ephesians, to be "a dwelling of God in the Spirit" (Eph. 2:20-22). In Jesus' community, people are intended to encounter the living God.

Pilgrims. For the author of the Epistle to the Hebrews, Christ's disciples are pilgrims journeying to a heavenly country. As the unseen God once called Abraham to leave his homeland and journey to an unknown land, God calls us in Christ to forsake the familiar securities of our own pasts and to follow Jesus to

a now-invisible destination and destiny in the world to come
(Heb. 11:8-16). Although we cannot see the object of our hope,
God has given us a taste of the heavenly gift and the powers
of the age to come, even allowing us to share in his Holy Spirit
(6:4-5). This is the same Spirit through whom God works miracles and gives gifts, according to his own will (2:4).

Even with divine power, however, lengthy travel with others wears hard on the nerves, and unforeseen hazards only
worsen the situation. When that happens, pilgrims can become
irritated with each other and discouraged in their journey. The
remedy, this author reminds, is keeping the eyes fixed on Jesus
(Heb. 12:2), tenderly caring for each other's needs (12:12-14),
and eliminating attitudes such as resentment, lust or covetous-
ness that poison community with God and with our travel com-
panions (12:14-17).

Peter also pictures disciples as resident aliens, en route to an
inheritance reserved for them in heaven, protected by God's
power through faith until they reach the goal (1 Pet. 1:1-5).

Family of God. The church is God's "household," writes
Paul to Timothy (1 Tim. 3:15). Christians are brothers and sisters, fathers and mothers in God's family. In that unity, they are
to live together in purity; the experienced ones teaching those
who are inexperienced by example and by word; and all serv-
ing one another (1 Tim. 3:1-13; 5:1-18).

Throughout his first epistle, John also addresses his converts as God's family, children of God, brothers and sisters to
one another. The sum of Christian life, writes this aged Apostle,
is to believe in Jesus Christ and to love each other. Through it
all, we know that Jesus is with us, for he has given us his Spirit
(1 John 3:24; 4:13).

Body of Christ. The most common New Testament metaphor for Jesus' community is that of the body of Christ, as pop-
ularized by the Apostle Paul. Just as the human body has many
members, each with different functions but all necessary to the

body's fullness, so individual believers are living members of Christ's spiritual body. Each member is important because God has positioned every one of them in the body. All members serve one another, according to God's individual gifting, for the common good. This means that no member is all-important and no member is useless (Rom. 12:4-8; 1 Cor. 12:12-27).

Just as the physical body is animated by living breath (spirit), without which it is dead, so Christ's spiritual body lives and functions in the power of the Holy Spirit. This is true of the individual Christian (Rom. 8:9-11). It is also true of the community as a whole (Eph 4:4).

In the New Testament, the figure of "member" always points to participation in Christ's spiritual body—never to membership in a club, society or even a religious institution. To be a member of Christ's body is to be a functioning part of a living, interdependent organism. The Bible never speaks of a "member of the church." Although Paul uses "church" and "body of Christ" interchangeably at times, the metaphor of "member" belongs with "body" and not with "church."

As a living organism, the body of Christ matures together, with each member making its own contribution toward that maturity. Power and direction come through the Holy Spirit from the head, which is Christ. The body's growth also comes from union with the head, again through the Holy Spirit. The goal of growth is maturity in its fullness, which means becoming completely like Christ himself (Eph. 4:11-16; Col. 2:19). Eventually, the body will share the destiny of its head, which is glory with God. God will bring about this result by his own power, again described as the Holy Spirit (Eph. 1:18-23; 3:20-21).

Paul calls members in Christ's body to the same community life envisioned by Jesus. They are to live holy lives, in union with Jesus himself (Col. 3:1-11). Theirs is a community notable for its compassion, kindness, humility, gentleness and patience (v. 12). They forgive each other, as Christ has forgiven them all (v. 13). They love one another, encourage each other, and live together in peace as the one body of Christ (v. 14-16). By word and action, they bring glory to God (v. 17). Motivated by gratitude, they are watchful in prayer, seeking opportunities to share the gospel graciously with outsiders as God opens doors (4:2-6).

The prophet Isaiah foretold the spiritual life of those whom the Messiah would save. "Everlasting joy will be theirs," he said, "and I will make an everlasting covenant with them." Each one of them will say: "I will rejoice greatly in the LORD, my soul will exult in my God; for He has clothed me with garments of salvation, he has wrapped me with a robe of righteousness."

Then, enlarging the prophetic view to include the entire messianic community on the earth, Isaiah continues: "For as the earth brings forth its sprouts, and as a garden causes the things sown in it to spring up, so the Lord GOD will cause righteousness and praise to spring up before all the nations" (Isa. 61:7-11).

Isaiah understood that human effort cannot produce such a life in community. A task this enormous requires the supernatural power of God. Yet such community does occur daily around the world—as it has in various places and times for nearly 2,000 years.

This community life is the fruit of the Holy Spirit (Gal. 5:22-23). It is an earthly sign of God's heavenly kingdom—the divine reign that is here already in embryonic form although its fullness remains for the future (Rom. 14:17). It means that Jesus is keeping his parting promise: "I am with you always, even to the end of the age" (Matt. 28:20).

The Spirit-filled community is one result of the Great Rescue, and a very important one at that. The fact is that God's kindness is so rich and diverse that it defies full description. Contemplating our Rescuer's grace is something like looking through a spiritual kaleidoscope.

Seventeen

THE KALEIDOSCOPE

In one sense, God's rescue of sinners is simple and straight-forward. We were in trouble. We could not help ourselves. God came in the person of Jesus and rescued us from sin and all its effects. We cannot improve on Jesus' work or add anything to it. By God's grace, we can trust in Jesus as our Savior and approach the Father based on what Jesus has done.

Whoever does trust Jesus in this way begins to live as a rescued person, enjoying God's forgiveness and all the benefits Jesus obtained on behalf of his people. A child can memorize and quote John 3:16, which summarizes this truth in one sentence, and millions of children have understood that sentence and claimed its reality for themselves.

But there is another sense is which the Great Rescue is complex and very profound. "As the heavens are higher than the earth," God reminded the prophet Isaiah, "so are My ways higher than your ways, and My thoughts than your thoughts" (Isa. 55:9). This same truth led the Apostle Paul to exclaim: "O the depth of the riches both of the wisdom and knowledge of God! How unsearchable are His judgments and unfathomable His ways!" (Rom. 11:33).

Not surprisingly, therefore, New Testament writers use an incredible variety of figures and illustrations to describe God's saving work and its happy results. It is as if the biblical writers handed us a spiritual kaleidoscope and invited us to have a look. If we peer into the viewer and rotate the instrument, a succession of wondrous images flashes before our eyes. Instead of symmetrical patterns created by mirrors and pieces of colored glass, however, this spiritual kaleidoscope is filled with metaphors for God's Great Rescue. Most of them, it turns out, are taken from the common activities of everyday life.

Tour of the Town

We may imagine the New Testament authors leading us on a tour of the town in search of suitable illustrations. As they guide us up one street and down the next, metaphors of salvation pop up everywhere we look.

Courthouse and law office. There is the courthouse, solemn and sedate. Inside the courtroom, a criminal stands before the judge, waiting to hear his verdict. Will the judge condemn this criminal and pronounce him guilty? Or will this defendant hear the words "Not guilty," and walk away free?

We, too, were guilty before the judge of the universe. We knew we were guilty—and God knew it, too. There was no hiding the fact, no pretending that matters were other than as they were. Despite that reality, God looked at Jesus Christ and acquitted us. He pronounced us righteous—not guilty—just as if we had never sinned. That is what it means to be "justified" (Rom. 3:24-26). Every time we see a courthouse we can remember that God does not treat us as we deserve but instead treats us far better.

Next door stands the attorney's office. We certainly need someone to speak on our behalf to the Creator of heavens and earth. To do that, God has provided Jesus Christ who died for us, rose again for us and now intercedes for us in heaven (Rom.

8:34). And while it is a mystery we cannot fully understand, Jesus is also with us on earth through the Holy Spirit, our divine Advocate (John 14:16).

Bank, baths, orphanage. Just a block over stands the bank. We were penniless in spiritual coin, this building reminds us, but Jesus became poor to make us rich (2 Cor. 8:9).

Three streets down we spot the public baths. These buildings prompt a thought we are happy to forget. Because of our sin, we once were filthy in God's eyes—nasty, foul and unclean. But in his mercy God cleansed us, washed us, made us spotless in his sight (1 Cor. 6:11).

Two blocks away we pass the orphanage. It also has meaning, for God has found us like abandoned orphans on the street. Then, prompted by a father's loving heart, God adopted us in union with Jesus Christ and made us his own dear children by grace (Eph. 1:5, 11).

Hospital, homes. Just around a curve the hospital comes into view. We were sick and broken in body, soul and spirit. But Jesus, the Great Physician, took our weaknesses and infirmities on himself. By his wounds, Jesus healed us in all aspects of our being—physical, emotional and spiritual alike (Matt. 8:17). That healing is not fully obvious yet, but Jesus promises that it will become clear to everyone before the Story is finished.

In the distance we see the roofs of cozy houses. Inside, parents laugh and love and children play. Our hearts fill with emotion at the sight. We know how precious is this blessing of home. For we once were homeless. Then the heavenly Father reconciled us in Jesus and called us home to live in his own family (Col. 1:20-22).

Inn, slave market. Beyond the residential section, on the public road stands the inn. Sojourners stop there to eat, to buy a refreshing drink, to rent a room and rest for the night. This facility, too, contributes a metaphor of our salvation. Like those sojourners, we ourselves are travelers through this life. We came to Jesus hungry, thirsty and tired. Jesus satisfied our hunger, filled us with living water and gave us rest in himself (Matt. 5:6; 11:28-30).

As we come to the edge of town, the countryside now in view, we find ourselves at a gloomy place—the market for human slaves. We shudder at the thought, for it brings back a dark and heavy memory. We were once slaves to sin ourselves, unable to resist its temptation no matter how hard we tried. Then Jesus set us free, at the cost of his own blood. God broke the chains of sin and empowered us to do what pleases him (Col. 1:14).

Cemetery. Beyond the slave market sprawls the cemetery. The grounds are still and quiet—and totally without hope for most who live in this town. Because of sin, we were dead as corpses before God. But for those who know Jesus, even this dreadful place fills us with gratitude and with praise. Because God was rich in mercy and full of love, he raised us to new life in Jesus and saved us by his grace (Eph. 2:1-7).

This place also reminds us that Jesus has conquered death, as shown by his own dying and rising from the tomb. What a change that made in our hearts! All our lives we lived in dread of dying, not knowing what, if anything, was on the other side (Heb. 2:14-15). But Jesus' resurrection turned on the light in the darkness. God is stronger than death—and Jesus is Exhibit Number One.

Even the word "cemetery" testifies to Jesus' resurrection. Before Christ, the Greeks normally called this place the *necropolis*—"the city of the dead." The gospel's influence gradually replaced that name with "cemetery," from a Greek word meaning "the sleeping place." All who are brought here as lifeless corpses will "wake up" one day, and those who now "sleep in Jesus" will rise to live with him forever (1 Thes. 4:13-17).

Common realities. All these figures share three truths in common. First, that our original condition was dreadful, gloomy and hopeless. Second, that those problems were self-inflicted through our own sinful attitudes and actions for which we had only ourselves to blame. Third, that God personally undertook the task of rescuing us—from our guilt and filth, our estrangement and bondage, our ailments and poverty, our hunger and thirst, our homelessness and all the rest—and he accomplished that Rescue without any help from us.

God did all this in the person of Jesus our representative. By the time we heard of it, it was already done. That being true, we cannot contribute anything to God's many-faceted salvation. All we can do is trust God's kind disposition toward us in his Son Jesus Christ and say "thank you" to God by our love, obedience and praise.

God's Work in Three Tenses

Our spiritual kaleidoscope not only shows us many scenes, it also portrays the Great Rescue in terms of past, present and future. Theologians like to speak, for example, of God's three great works of justification, sanctification and glorification. As a general rule, these words describe salvation in three tenses. As believers, we may say: "I have been justified; I am being sanctified; I will be glorified." If we look at these three words carefully, we can see God's saving work done yesterday, the saving work he is doing today and the work of salvation that God will do tomorrow—at the Last Day.

Justification. Justification is God's past work for us. In justification, God delivers us from sin's penalty (Rom. 5:9). Our experience of justification occurs at the beginning of the Christian life, when one comes to Christ in faith. It is God's verdict of acquittal in our salvation—his pronouncement, for Jesus' sake, that we are not guilty in his sight. In God's plan, every true believer has been justified.

(As we saw in an earlier chapter, God gave his verdict on Christ's people when he issued his verdict on Jesus Christ our representative. But as we also saw, what happened objectively in Jesus, we enjoy subjectively by faith after we hear the gospel news.)

Sanctification. Sanctification is God's present work in us. In sanctification, God delivers us from sin's power (1 Thes. 4:3, 7). Sanctification occurs throughout the Christian life, as one lives in relation with Christ by faith. It is God's transforming work in our salvation—his enabling us, through the Holy Spirit, to become more and more like Jesus our Lord. In God's plan, every true believer is being sanctified.

(As with justification, Scripture sometimes speaks of our having been sanctified, or made holy, in the doing and dying of Jesus our head. However, in the New Testament sanctification usually refers to God's applying to our own personal experience the reality he accomplished for us in Jesus.)

Glorification. Glorification is God's future work on us. In glorification, God will deliver us from sin's presence and make us unable to sin (Rom. 8:17-19). Glorification will occur at the conclusion of the Christian life, when we welcome back our Savior from heaven. It is God's crowning work for his people. Then he will give us bodies that are deathless and pain-free. We will see Jesus as he is—and we will be like him. We will share his glory—the glory that he now enjoys as our representative and head. In God's plan, every true believer will be glorified.

(Even glorification is a finished work in the mind of God, who sees the end from the beginning. We use the word in its normal sense, however, to describe the perfected state awaiting God's people in the Age to Come.)

Grace from Eternity to Eternity

Sometimes Christians think about salvation in a very narrow and limited way. When they do that, they focus on one aspect of salvation—perhaps God's justification, or verdict of acquittal—and ignore or overlook all other aspects. For example, some people almost always speak of salvation in the past tense—referring to when they "got saved."

The New Testament writers do speak of salvation in the past tense. Christians are people who have been saved (Eph. 2:8). But the Bible also speaks of those who are "being" saved (1 Cor. 1:18). And it says that we "shall be saved" in the Last Day (Rom. 5:9-10). If we think only about God's past work, we will miss the excitement of watching his activity throughout our Christian lives and the joy of anticipating his ultimate work in the future.

Other Christians are quite sure that God will save his faithful people at the End, but they seem almost totally unaware that he already has pronounced them "not guilty" in the past. These Christians emphasize their hope for the future. But without the assurance that comes from knowing God's gracious verdict in the past, hope easily melts into wishful thinking and finally dissolves into hopelessness. Such Christians lack confidence concerning their salvation now, and they are afraid that they will not be among those who enjoy it when Jesus returns. They need a strong dose of gospel tonic to revive their sagging spirits.

Other aspects. The Bible speaks in three tenses concerning other aspects of the Great Rescue. We have been redeemed or liberated by Jesus' blood (Eph. 1:7). But that is not the end of the Story. We also look forward to the day of redemption (Eph. 1:14). We have been washed and cleansed in the past (1 Cor. 6:11). Yet the Christian life involves continual cleansing (1 John 1:7). The Messiah came, and he is yet to come (Heb. 9:26, 28). The Kingdom is here but it is also coming, and Jesus taught us to pray that it will come on earth as it is in heaven (Matt. 6:10).

An Eternal Program of Grace

"With all this talk about past, present and future," you might ask, "when am I actually saved?" It is a reasonable question, to which the Bible's answer is: from eternity to eternity. God's kindness to sinners through Jesus Christ is far too massive and rich to write in one day's calendar space. Much less will it fit an appointment slot on a daily agenda.

To mark the grace of God, we need to draw a golden line from the beginning of each day to its end ... from one week and month to the next ... through all the calendars of all our years—and all the other years that went before us and all those that will come after we are gone.

Salvation involves not only our past, present and future. It began in the mind of God before time itself, and it will extend into the everlasting ages after earthly time has ended. God's Great Rescue from sin stretches from eternity to eternity. It is the unfolding and actualization of an eternal program of grace. The Apostle Paul lays out this grand vision in Romans chapter 8. Let us follow him step by step beginning with verse 17.

Groans of childbirth. In this world we encounter many difficulties that we simply cannot understand, the Apostle begins. We can immediately compose a list of our own. Faithful people sometimes waste away with painful diseases. Godly men and women die young. Haughty individuals who ignore and blaspheme God take advantage of others who love and serve God with all their hearts. Sometimes, as in Paul's day—and in many countries today—ungodly rulers persecute Christians simply because they trust in Jesus Christ and invite others to do the same (Rom. 8:17-18).

Paul's heart resonated with the suffering cries of godly people. But he also heard another sound—a tortured groan rising from the depths of the whole created order. It is the sound of labor, he said. Creation is groaning in childbirth—anxiously waiting for Jesus to redeem it from the bondage and futility of sin (v. 19-22). Even though God's people have the Holy Spirit, they also groan for redemption—waiting eagerly for bodies that will not sin or suffer or die ever again (v. 23-25).

God works for good. Surrounded by a broken world, frustrated by sin, anxious to experience the fullness of our salvation, we often open our mouths to cry out to God, only to discover that we lack the words. "We do not know how to pray as we should," Paul explains. At such times, God's Spirit in us takes up our slack, fills in our gaps, interceding for us to God with "groanings" too deep for words (v. 26). When we cannot express our deepest feelings, God hears the Spirit's intercession, which matches God's own desires (v. 27).

Although we often do not know how to pray, Paul next tells us something that we do know for sure. "We know that God causes all things to work together for good to those who love God, to those who are called according to His purpose" (v. 28). For all those who now endure what Paul calls "the sufferings of this present time," this is a precious verse indeed. Truly, even the sufferings of faithful people are in the hands of God in whom they trust. God can bring good from all that we experience as bad.

All things. All that is true, but Paul is making an even larger point in this passage. The Apostle is looking beyond time—from eternity to eternity. On that vast screen, Paul sees a reality that is almost too good to believe. The sovereign God is personally at work from eternity to eternity for the salvation of his people—whom Paul here describes as "those who love God and who are called according to his purpose."

In verses 29 and 30 of Romans 8, Paul identifies the "all things" that God is "working together" for our good. The phrase "working together" translates a Greek word that gives our verb "synergize." This coordinated divine activity begins before the first verse of Genesis and it continues beyond the final verse of Revelation. As we observe the Great Rescue from eternity to eternity, we see God act on behalf of his people in five great scenes.

Scene 1 — God foreknew them (v. 29). This scene and the next take place before God made the world or even time itself.

In biblical usage, to "know" someone is to experience a relationship with that person. In this first scene, God sets his love on all who finally will be saved, long before they are even born. He chooses (or "elects") them for fellowship with himself. He gives them to the Son of God, who would later be born as the man Jesus of Nazareth. Although God's people will choose him during the course of their lives, an idea to which we will return, what we see in Scene 1 always reminds us that God chose them first.

Scene 2 — God predestined that they should become like Christ (v. 29). This text does not suggest some kind of fatalism that removes our responsibility and personal choices. Nor is Paul saying here that every detail of our lives is determined in advance. Instead the Apostle assures us that God has predetermined that all who belong to him will finally resemble Jesus Christ his beloved Son in moral character.

Scene 3 — God called them (v. 30). This scene is filled with invitations, addressed to all of God's people and requesting that they reply to God himself. The heavenly Father invites his people to know him, to live in relationship with him, and finally to live with him forever. Since the Great Rescuer came and saved his people from their sins, God's invitation comes to people in the form of the gospel message—the good news of everything that God has accomplished in the person of Jesus Christ.

Scene 4 — God justified them (v. 30). In this scene we see God sitting as judge in his heavenly courtroom. He is saying to an accused person: "I find you not guilty." Because Jesus took the place of his people in his obedience and in his suffering, God acquits or declares "not guilty" all those whom Jesus represents—even though they all are truly guilty and deserve to be punished.

Scene 5 — God glorified them (v. 30). This scene is still future, but it is so certain that Paul describes it as past. Here we see God at the place where this world intersects with the Age to Come. He is miraculously perfecting them for eternity, making them exactly like Jesus. And he is giving them bodies that are fitted to the Age to Come—bodies that will never be sick or die again.

The same people throughout. God coordinates and accomplishes all these things for the good of everyone who loves him in response to his invitation. The same people who are in any one of these scenes are in all the other scenes as well. These are not random acts of God—he works them all together. Each work of God leads to the next. He sees the end from the beginning, and he is faithful to finish whatever he starts (Phil. 1:6).

If we wonder whether we are included in Scenes 1 and 2 (which took place before the world began), and if we will be in Scene 5 (which will happen at the End), we need only to see whether we are in Scenes 3 and 4 (which God carries out in the course of our own lives here and now). If God effectively called us by the gospel, for example, we may know that he also chose us before the world began (1 Thes. 1:4-5; 2 Thes. 2:13-14). If God is transforming us, however slowly, into the likeness of Jesus Christ, we may be sure that God has called us and chosen us as well (2 Pet. 1:10).

This does not mean that we never sin, or that we always do our best. It does mean that when we sin, the Holy Spirit lets us know about it by convicting our consciences. It means that we are sorry when we displease God, and that we really desire, deep inside, to make him happy. The person who loves God and is invited according to his plan wants to do what is right. That person enjoys God's company and is delighted at the thought of spending eternity face to face with the heavenly Father and with Jesus Christ his Son.

All of grace. Salvation is not mostly by grace. It is totally by grace from first to last. This truth is so marvelous that it catches even many Christians by surprise. Perhaps it is helpful to begin at the end and to work backward. Let us mark it down, therefore, that the "elect"—those whom God "foreknew"—are the exact same people who finally will join Jesus in glory. (They comprise an enormous multitude, by the way. Revelation 7:9 says their number is too large to count.) We will have no doubt, when we view Scene 5, that their glorification is based totally on grace. They do not deserve any of it. God does not glorify them because of any merit he sees in them.

The same is true of their justification in Scene 4. God declares these people righteous, "not guilty," totally as a matter of grace. They do not deserve to be acquitted of sin. God does not pronounce them righteous because of any merit he sees in them. We may say the same of their calling in Scene 3. God does not invite people who deserve to be invited. He invites sinners who do not deserve an invitation. God's invitation is not based on merit. It is based solely on his grace.

So it is with God's determination to transform sinners into the likeness of Jesus. God does not take applications for his work in Scene 2. He does not sort resumes to see who deserves to be made into the image of Christ. This divine work flows totally from God's grace—not from human merit.

God's saving work in Scene 1 is equally the result of divine grace, out of which God "foreknew" or (in parallel texts such as Ephesians 1:3-14, 2 Thessalonians 2:13-14 and 1 Peter 1:1-4) "chose" his people in Christ before the world began. Salvation is "not according to our works, but according to God's own purpose and grace which was granted us in Christ Jesus from all eternity" (2 Tim. 1:9). God did not look into the future to see who deserved to be chosen, just as he will not look into the past at the End to see who deserves to be glorified. God works all these things because of who he is, not because of who we are.

Human responsibility and divine grace. The Bible does not encourage us to think of God's choosing in terms of a cosmic roulette wheel. Scripture never blames God for not choosing those who are finally lost. Those who are finally lost will find themselves in that condition because they rejected God and his grace. For that they are totally and solely to blame. Election is not about the lost. It is about the saved. It shines like a spot-lighted banner from before the creation of the world, a banner on which are written the words—"Salvation is totally by grace!"

The gospel is to be proclaimed to all. Everyone is command-ed to repent and to believe the gospel. People make responsi-ble choices and they are accountable for the choices they make. We see this illustrated in the reactions of those who heard Paul preach in a synagogue in Pisidian Antioch. Some who were present believed the gospel when they heard it. Luke describes them as those who "were appointed to eternal life" (Acts 13:48). Others rejected the gospel and refused to believe. Paul tells them that they have judged themselves unworthy of eternal life (Acts 13:46).

We cannot fully explain God's gracious election and human accountability. However, we can believe both truths—for Scripture teaches them both. Each truth serves its own impor-tant purpose. Perhaps we may think of it like this. On the road of conversion there is a gate. On the outside of the gate is a sign that announces: "Whosoever will may come!" Only those who enter through the gate see the other side. There they see anoth-er sign that affirms: "Chosen from the foundation of the world!"

These are profound truths that raise questions we cannot fully answer in this life. Paul did not write these verses to tease our intellect or to create an argument. He wrote them to bolster our faith, to stimulate our praise and thanksgiving to God who rescued us. "What shall we say to these things?" Paul finally asks. The answer is clear, and all believers can sing it in happy unison together—"If God is for us, who is against us?" (Rom. 8:31).

God *is* for us, the gospel shouts, and at this point we have only begun to see how much. To experience the fullness of God's never-ending love, we will have to wait for the grand finale.

Eighteen

THE GRAND FINALE

Stories and the Story

For as long as anyone can remember, human beings have tried to make sense of brokenness—the brokenness they have experienced in themselves and have observed throughout their world. Sages have thought, mystics have meditated, scholars have researched and reflected. Very often, these all have then told stories—grand, over-arching stories that envelop all of human history and even reach beyond—in an effort to explain the inevitable questions of "How?" and "Why?" and "So what?"

Such stories have given birth to world religions. These religions, in turn, have shaped entire cultures. And those cultures have produced literature and arts, cultivated moralities and, from a human standpoint, turned the course of history. The Bible's Story, which we have briefly surveyed in this book, provides one such explanation. But it stands apart from the other stories in at least three important respects.

A unique story. First of all, this Story begins and ends with the living God who is both infinite and personal. Only stories based on the Bible have such a God as that. The gods of Greek and Roman mythology, for example, were personal but far from infinite. They struggled with all the limitations of character—and even the limitations of power—that we do. The gods of Hinduism and Buddhism, on the other hand, are sometimes portrayed as infinite but they are far from personal in any meaningful sense. The Bible portrays God the eternal and almighty Creator who became a human being and lived as one of us.

The second distinction is that, in the Bible, God himself reveals the Story. From the opening verses of Genesis to the final words of Revelation, God does powerful deeds—then he explains what he has done and what it means for his people. The Bible does not tell a story of humans searching for God until they find him. It records the tale of God who seeks out his errant human creatures and brings them back to himself.

The third unique aspect about the Bible's Story is that, unlike other stories, which have no living God who is in charge—and which therefore go around and around in circles with no foreseeable end—this Story moves to a grand conclusion.

This Story not only moves from a beginning to an end in terms of earthly time and history. It also "moves" in the sense that all the scenes connect, from the first one to the final one. In this Story, what comes later relates to what has gone before. The Story opens with God and ends with God. It begins with a sin-free universe and it closes the same way. Throughout this entire Story, the God who acts at its beginning and at its end continues to direct the action, resolving the conflict created by human sin, moving the Story from an earth-time stage to an eternal dimension.

The Big Picture

The big picture is absolutely clear, though Christians still struggle to understand some of the details. From the beginning, Christian believers have proclaimed that the same Jesus who for our sake was crucified under Pontius Pilate, who rose from the dead and ascended into heaven to sit at God's right hand, "will come again in glory to judge the living and the dead, and his kingdom will have no end" (to borrow words from the ancient Nicene Creed).

Beyond that, the Bible says surprisingly little about the conclusion of the Story. When the biblical writers do talk about the finale, they often speak in an understated manner. It is as if we ought to know that, in this Story, these things follow quite naturally—and also that we really need very few details at this stage on our journey.

John's Gospel. John is content in his Gospel, for example, to inform believers that they have eternal life, that they have overcome death and that they will never perish. Moreover, this eternal life has started already. It is "eternal" in nature or quality, as well as in duration. This life does not originate with the present world, and it is not limited to our present bounds of time and space. It is life of the Age to Come. Most of all, eternal life means knowing God and his Son, Jesus Christ (John 17:3).

Paul. Paul also provides some specific glimpses into the Age to Come. Yet he considers it enough to tell his converts at Ephesus that, in the coming ages, God will continue to "show the surpassing riches of His grace in kindness toward us in Christ Jesus" (Eph. 2:7). We will be in God's hands. He loves us. And he has only started, in this present life, to show us just how much! Whatever the details, the adventures that await us beyond the resurrection will be good and joyful and consistent with the blessings God has begun to pour out on us already for the sake of Jesus Christ.

Peter. Our eternal future, Peter suggests, is too wonderful for our present limited minds to understand. Instead of trying to describe its wonder and beauty in positive terms, therefore, he tells us what it is not. The inheritance now reserved in heaven for God's people is "imperishable and undefiled and will not fade away" (1 Pet. 1:4).

Everything we treasure here, everything we now enjoy, is just the opposite. However grand, all earthly treasures finally will perish. However precious and pure, all that is earthly can be soiled and scarred and marred. No matter how bright and permanent it now appears, everything that is beautiful in this life will one day fade away.

So Peter asks us to visualize the most beautiful scenes imaginable, to think of the most wondrous and precious treasures our minds can conjure. He invites us to erase from those pictures everything that detracts or spoils or compromises their perfection—then to imagine all these scenes and treasures lasting forever. And that is only a hint of the eternal inheritance God has prepared—a future for which every believer has a personal reservation.

Specific Imagery

In addition to these hints, biblical writers also use a multitude of figures to impress us with specific benefits of the Great Rescue that await God's people on the other side of death and the resurrection.

The Kingdom of God. For Gospel writers other than John, it is enough to say that God's people will finally participate in the kingdom of God, or as Matthew reverently describes it, the kingdom of heaven. This imagery is packed with meaning for everyone familiar with the Old Testament (you might wish to turn back now and re-read the section of chapter 8 in this book titled "Still More to Come"). It was also Jesus' favorite way of talking about the blessed future. According to Matthew's Gospel, those who inherit the kingdom of heaven will enjoy eternal life as God's final reward. God will gather them to himself and they will inherit the earth.

Union with God and Christ. New Testament authors frequently describe the believer's final state in terms of his or her relationship with God the Father and with his Son, Jesus Christ.

Those who are faithful to Jesus now may look forward to his return, when he will personally acknowledge them in the presence of his Father (Matt. 10:32). God's people will be with Jesus forever (John 14:1-3; 1 Thes. 4:7). They will see Jesus in his full splendor (1 Cor. 1:7-8).

More than that, God will make them like Jesus (1 John 3:2). Over and again, Paul promises his readers that they will share Christ's glory or splendor when he comes again (Col. 3:4; 2 Thes. 1:10; 2:14). This apparently has a moral aspect and a physical aspect as well. Based on Jesus' accomplishments in their stead, God will receive a people who are holy (Col. 1:22) and blameless (Jude 24). The suggestion is also that God will then perfect his process of sanctification, removing every trace of the fallen nature from his people so that they will never again be tempted to sin. (Besides that, the old Tempter will also be gone, which provides a double guarantee!)

Jesus will also fashion his people into the likeness of his own glorified, resurrected body (Phil. 3:20-21). Paul says that it is folly to ask too many questions about this subject. However, in 1 Corinthians 15:35-58, he reveals a number of striking details. Our body now, he notes, becomes injured and can be eaten away by disease (corruptible). Most of us are not particularly beautiful, and some of us suffer deformities or other bodily afflictions (dishonorable). All of our bodies now have limitations of strength (weak), of nature (fleshly), of origin (earthly) and of endurance (mortal).

Our eternal body, however, will share none of these restrictions, limitations or liabilities. A list of its characteristics conjures a quality of life that we now can scarcely imagine. Try to filter this group of adjectives through your imagination as you contemplate such a person—*incorruptible, honorable, powerful, spiritual, heavenly, immortal, deathless.* One thing is certain: you will still be you and I will still be me. Just as our present body provides the channels for us to relate to this creation, so our eternal-model body will equip us to enjoy the universe that will last forever.

Creation's purpose fulfilled. We said earlier that the conclusion of the Bible's story relates to its beginning. This means, among other things, that the grand finale for God's people will be the fulfillment or realization of creation as God originally intended it—an intent which sin has temporarily delayed. Jesus speaks of that final state as "the regeneration" (Matt. 19:28). Peter calls it "the restoration of all things" spoken by the ancient prophets (Acts 3:21).

Paul portrays creation groaning now, waiting to be redeemed from its present bondage to corruption (Rom. 8:19-21). He describes this state as the "summing up of all things in Christ" in heaven and on earth (Eph. 1:10). He speaks of it as the "perfect" or complete state of affairs (1 Cor. 13:10). Just as our bodies will be changed, so God will transform and renew his creation. "Behold, I make all things new," he announces to John in the Patmos vision (Rev. 21:5). He does not say, "I make all new things." Creation's original purpose will be fully realized when Jesus returns.

Newness. "Something old; something new," goes the traditional bridal saying. At the wedding feast of Christ and his church, there will also be something old—though redeemed and totally transformed—and something new. The author of Hebrews encourages his readers to look forward to the "world to come" (Heb. 2:5). In other passages, he narrows the focus to "a better country" (11:6), or to a "city to come" (13:14). Whether you relish city-dwelling or life in the country, there will be blessings enough to satisfy and to gratify you forever in the Age to Come.

Peter promises "new heavens and a new earth" filled with nothing but righteousness (2 Pet. 3:13). In biblical symbolism, this expression points to a whole new universe. There will be plenty for God's people to do throughout eternity—and room enough to do it all.

The last word. John gives the Bible's most detailed description of the grand finale in Revelation chapters 21-22. There the aged Apostle stands open-mouthed in amazement at the sight of new heaven and new earth—a new universe, God's fresh creation designed for all eternity (21:1).

As John watches, heaven opens and from it there comes down the new Jerusalem, a holy city (21:2). The final reward is not haloed harp-playing in isolation on a lonely cloud but holy fellowship in society with all the redeemed. This is a diverse population, rescued from all nations throughout earthly time—all bringing with them everything that is good and that glorifies God (21:24).

The Story finally ends as it began. The curse that once fell on earth and its inhabitants is forever gone (22:3). The Tree of Life, once placed off-limits to human beings at the point of a flaming sword, is again planted within easy reach of all (22:2). The River of the Water of Life flows from God's throne. Its stream both adorns and waters this new creation. Abundant life springs up wherever it flows (22:1-2).

The glory of God illuminates this scene, but this glory is not contained in a Temple (21:11). No Temple is needed, because God and Jesus are here (21:22-23). God's people now see him face to face (22:4). In his returned pure gaze of divine love, they experience the communion of spirit for which they were made. The rescued universe reverberates with shouts of praise and joy.